*The Emperor Horikawa Diary*

# The Emperor Horikawa Diary

by Fujiwara no Nagako
*Sanuki no Suke Nikki*

Translated with an Introduction by
Jennifer Brewster

The University Press of Hawaii
Honolulu

Library of Congress Catalog Card Number 77-89194
ISBN 0-8248-0605-0

Simultaneously published by Australian National University Press
as *Sanuki no Suke Nikki*

Manufactured in Australia at
Griffin Press Limited, Marion Road, Netley, South Australia

for Christopher, David and Helen

# PREFACE

*Sanuki no Suke Nikki* is a journal in two books, written by Fujiwara no Nagako, an Assistant Attendant in the Palace Attendants' Office during the reigns of Emperor Horikawa (1086–1107) and of his son, Emperor Toba (1107–1123). The first book describes the deteriorating state of health of Emperor Horikawa, and his death on the nineteenth day of the seventh month, 1107. The second book begins with the recall of the authoress to court in the tenth month of 1107, and the last definite date given is the last day of 1108. While recording the various ceremonies concerned with the accession of Emperor Toba, this book's primary concern is with Horikawa's character, and of aspects of his relationship with the authoress.

*Sanuki no Suke Nikki* is a late Heian example of the genre of diaries with literary merit, or *nikki bungaku*, a genre already well-known through translations of *Kagerō Nikki*, *Izumi Shikibu Nikki* and *Sarashina Nikki*. Nevertheless, while continuing in the literary tradition of such works, *Sanuki no Suke Nikki* does not equal them in literary merit. Rather it is as an historical source that its value lies, especially in that it stems from the early *insei* period, when the imperial family was trying to re-organise its internal structure in order to hold its own among the other powerful families of the day. While Emperor Horikawa, the central figure of *Sanuki no Suke Nikki*, left little mark in Japanese history, the favourable picture of him that emerges in this diary may help to explain why this early period of *insei* was not troubled by the intra- and inter-family feuds that were a feature of the later period. In its depiction of court life, customs and religious attitudes, *Sanuki no Suke Nikki* has considerable value also as a social document for the period.

*Sanuki no Suke Nikki* seems to have enjoyed an initial popularity in the Kamakura period, but thereafter slipped into oblivion, and was virtually ignored until the decade before World War II, when it was rediscovered by Tamai Kōsuke who, after establishing the authorship of the work in an article published in 1929, went on to produce the first annotated text in 1936. There has been a resurgence of interest in the work in recent years, probably because its portrayal of the emperor as a benevolent yet very human figure reflects to some degree present universal trends towards a recasting of monarchal roles.

This translation is based on an earlier doctoral thesis, which used as its basic text Tamai Kōsuke's annotated text, published by the Asahi Shimbunsha in 1964 in the *Nihon koten zensho* series, and based primarily on the *Gunsho ruijū* manuscript. Extensive revisions have, however, been made in the light of Ishii Fumio's annotated text published by the Shogakukan in 1971 in vol. XVIII of the *Nihon koten bungaku zenshū* series. This text is based primarily on the *Kinshidō* manuscript from the Ise Shrine Collection, but takes into account recent scholarship on the work, in particular that of Katagiri Yō'ichi, Imakōji Kakuzui and Mitani Sachiko. There remain, nevertheless, several passages the meaning of which is still obscure. In all but one instance a translation has been attempted, in order to maintain the flow of the work, but such passages have been noted.

# ACKNOWLEDGMENTS

I should like to thank Professor Joyce Akroyd of the University of Queensland and Dr R. L. Backus of the University of California at Santa Barbara for introducing me to this work; Professor E. S. Crawcour and Dr R. H. P. Mason for their kind direction and encouragement; Professor M. Hiramatsu of Keiō University and Professor Y. Uehara for their helpful comments on the translation; Miss Sachiko Mitani, of the Sōai Gakuen at Osaka, for material and advice; and all those in the Faculty of Asian Studies and the Australian National University Library who, in innumerable ways, have offered their assistance. I should also like to thank my husband, without whose constant encouragement this work would never have been completed. Finally, thanks are due the Publications Committee of the Faculty of Asian Studies, Australian National University, for assistance in the publication of this work.

Canberra 1976.                                                      J.B.

# CONTENTS

# INTRODUCTION

*Sanuki no Suke Nikki* in its present form consists of two books. Book One opens with a prologue written in the fifth month of an unspecified year, in which the authoress, Fujiwara no Nagako, explains that her aim in writing is to try to alleviate, by putting her memories to paper, her sorrow over the death of Emperor Horikawa, whom she had served for eight years.

She then moves straight into her narrative, describing the early symptoms of Horikawa's illness, which started on the twentieth day of the sixth month 1107. This first book concentrates on the worsening condition of the Emperor, the Buddhist ceremonies held for his recovery, the two visits paid him by the Empress, and the appearance of an evil spirit. Tension mounts with the administration of the Buddhist vows by the Master of the Buddhist Law, Kensen, and the reading of the sutras by the Emperor's uncle, the Holy Teacher Jōkai. The climax comes with the death of the Emperor on the nineteenth day of the seventh month, at the age of only twenty-nine, and the complete breakdown of his attendants. The book ends rather abruptly with the removal of the Sacred Sword and Jewel to the palace of the Crown Prince.

Book One was probably written from notes made soon after the event. It is highly improbable that Nagako, exhausted as she was from her long vigils over the dying Emperor, would have found the time or energy to make regular diary-type entries, but it is likely that she filled in the empty hours at home after the Emperor's death by making some sort of record. This is borne out by the paucity of dates in her narrative. The main concern of Nagako and the others tending the Emperor was whether they could nurse him through each crisis, and consequently the emphasis is on the passage of time within each day, and especially on the approach of dawn, rather than on the actual date.

> As it drew towards dawn, I heard the sound of the temple bells. Dawn must be about to break, I thought joyfully, and then at last I heard the cawing of the crows. The sounds made by the early morning cleaners confirmed me in my impression that dawn had finally broken, and I was glad.

Book Two hinges on Nagako's recall to court, in the tenth month of 1107, to serve Horikawa's five year old son Toba, who reigned from 1107 to 1123, and then served as Retired Emperor to his death in 1156. A large part of this book is concerned with court functions such as Toba's accession ceremony, his move to the Imperial Palace, and the Great Festival of Thanksgiving and its related functions. However, it contains on the whole material of a more personal nature than Book One. Its most important theme is the treatment, by the method of flashbacks, of Horikawa's character and of various aspects of his relationship with Nagako. Thus, the sight of a palace building or piece of furniture, or the preparations for a certain annual festival, will launch the authoress into a flood of memories about the past. Her usual technique is to record one anecdote about the past for each month of the year, the anecdote generally taking precedence over the account of the contemporary situation.

The main part of Book Two concludes with Nagako's visit to the Palace to assist in the New Year ceremonies for 1107. Then follows a form of apology for her work, a description of a visit, in the tenth month of an unspecified year, to the Kōryūji where Horikawa's ashes were kept; an exchange of five poems, the final two of which seem to serve as a poetic conclusion to the work; and a final passage, rather in the form of an epilogue, describing how Nagako invited a person known as Lady Hitachi to be the first to see her completed work.

Book Two provides a complete contrast to Book One, not only in its anecdotal and reflective treatment, but also in its use of various literary devices. The most striking of these is the inclusion of poetry, Book Two containing twenty-three poems, whereas Book

One has none. The majority of these poems are by Nagako herself, but several other poets are quoted, or their poems reworked, on occasions when the sentiments expressed in the poem, or the circumstances of its composition, parallel Nagako's own.

The inclusion of these poems suggests that Nagako was aided in the writing of Book Two by a *shikashū*, or private anthology of poems. Such anthologies were usually compiled from old letters, drafts of poems, and poems copied from imperial or private anthologies, fans and screens. The compilation was usually effected by the poet himself, though there exist many examples of *shikashū* written in the third person. Some prefatory or concluding lines often disclaim any literary aspirations for the work, but in fact great care usually went into such anthologies, for they were one of the main sources utilised by compilers of imperial anthologies (*chokusenshū*). Many private anthologies were divided into the same categories used in the imperial anthologies—spring, summer, autumn, winter, love, parting, miscellaneous—while others were arranged in chronological order. As it was usual to include a brief note, known as *kotobagaki*, on the circumstances of a poem's composition, the dividing line between a private anthology and a *nikki*, diary or memoir, is often hard to establish.

Another device, which often stems from reliance on a private anthology, is the use of poetic allusions, whereby a phrase from a poem is incorporated in a prose passage. This technique lends itself best to reflective passages, and is employed throughout Book Two, though it is most obvious at the beginning and end of the book. The same technique is employed in the prologue to Book One, suggesting that Nagako, on some occasion when she found time heavy on her hands, took up the notes she had made subsequent to Horikawa's death, and decided to make them part of a more comprehensive work.

The first part was probably left much as it was, apart from the addition of the prologue, which is obviously intended to impress the reader with the literary skills of the writer. Fortunately Nagako seems to have realised that the fairly short, abrupt sentences of her original, and the extensive use of direct speech, increased the impact of her narrative of impending death, and so added nothing to detract from this central theme. At most, the reader is asked to imagine for himself the feelings of those tending the Emperor.

Book Two, with its anecdotal treatment and scattering of poems and poetic allusions, suggests a fairly leisurely composition. This affords the authoress the opportunity to fill out certain characters or incidents she had glossed over only briefly in Book One. Some measure of the contrast in style between the two books is afforded by a comparison of an incident in which the Emperor shielded Nagako from the eyes of the Regent by bending up his knees. This considerate action made a great impression on her, and she refers to it in all three times. In Book One she writes:

> When the Regent came close, the Emperor drew up his knees, hiding me behind them. Lying there beneath an unlined robe, I heard the Regent say . . .

The same incident is retold as follows in Book Two:

> On one such occasion the Regent approached from behind. I rose, and was about to withdraw, as I felt that it would be ill-mannered and unseemly to remain lying where I was, when the Emperor, realising that I must be feeling that I should not be seen, said 'Stay where you are. I shall make a screen.' He bent up his knees, and hid me behind them.

The flashback technique developed in Book Two provided Nagako with a unique and very effective means of character portrayal, for it enabled her to pinpoint any facet of character she chose, and make it the key to a brief one-act drama. The result may be accused of bias, and a lack of unity or cohesion, but what it loses on these counts it more than makes up for in its dramatic impact. Where else can one read of an Emperor pasting flute music to the Palace walls as an *aide-memoir*, personally arranging the sleeve-openings of the ladies-in-waiting for the Chrysanthemum Festival, sticking out his tongue and fleeing when he hears who is to serve his meal?

The success of the technique tends to be confined to the Emperor, as Nagako makes no effort to enlarge on any other character, and is rather too self-conscious to achieve an effective self-portrait. The impression of aloofness and introspection conveyed by Book One is reinforced by Book Two, and in general her attempts at self-analysis are so tied to Buddhist notions of *karma* and rebirth as to throw little light on her personality. It is only occasionally, in some of the dramatic flashback interludes, that one has a glimpse of that independence of spirit which must have appealed to the Emperor—the spontaneous reaction of disappointment in the game of fan-lottery, the choice of a different coloured robe from everyone else at the Chrysanthemum Festival, the refusal to be moved by the Emperor's feigned illness. It is almost as if Nagako only came to life in the presence of the Emperor.

The rather fragmented passages at the end of both books, combined with some obscure or apparently irrelevant passages in the body of each book, suggest that parts of the work have been lost. Substance is given this by by the *Honchō Shojaku Mokuroku*, a thirteenth century catalogue of literary works, which lists *Sanuki no Suke Nikki* as consisting of three books.[1] This entry has aroused much speculation as to the original form of the work. The most likely solution is that the missing book, if it existed, was placed originally between the two extant books. The grounds for this assumption are the abrupt ending of Book One with a passage which is both textually corrupt and chronologically misplaced, and the strange omission of any mention of Horikawa's funeral and forty-ninth day ceremony, including the distribution of mourning clothes. The strangeness of this omission is emphasised by a passage in the present Book Two, which suggests that Nagako had in fact already written of the forty-ninth day ceremony:

> When the day of the anniversary of Emperor Horikawa's death arrived, the ceremonies were conducted by one hundred priests, just as for the forty-ninth day ceremony last year. As the proceedings were the same, I shall not describe them.

Nagako also writes of the Kōryūji, and of those who were given mourning clothes to wear, as if these had already been mentioned. Then again, her description of a visit to a temple in the second month of 1108 seems to have no relevance at all to the main theme, while in her concluding remarks, she writes rather cryptically:

Those who happen to read this may well be critical, and say 'It is unpleasant to find a mere lady-in-waiting giving herself such knowledgeable airs.' However, even in the case of the discussions on the Buddhist sutras, this was the sort of topic the late Emperor had been wont to bring up for my edification during the course of our conversations on various matters. I have just described things as I remember them. Nobody should be critical of that.

On grounds of style, also, it would seem most likely that any missing book was placed between the existing two books. There is an obvious attempt at symmetry between the prologue and sections 52 and 54. In both, Nagako sets forth her aims in writing, while her poem in section 54 echoes a sentiment expressed in the prologue. Both the prologue and section 52 contain a large proportion of literary allusions, and both are concluded with the terminal particle *zo*, commonly used to mark the end of a section. The epilogue itself was evidently added after the completed work had been shown to Lady Hitachi, but the poems in section 54 could well once have constituted a final exchange between Nagako and this lady, thus making more effective the repetition of the sentiment in the prologue and the final poem.

It is interesting that some of the more obscure passages in *Sanuki no Suke Nikki*, such as Emperor Horikawa's attempts to teach Nagako the sutras, and the description of a visit to a temple in the second month, as well as the strangest of the omissions, the funeral and forty-ninth day ceremony, are all matters related to Buddhism. Nagako herself, as seen above, seems to have been worried that her work would be criticised on grounds of pedantry, especially in respect to references to Buddhism. It is quite possible that her work came into the hands of the great poet Fujiwara no Sadaie, who was the great-grandson of her sister Kaneko. Sadaie devoted much time to editing Heian and early Kamakura period literary works, and he may have been inclined to agree with Nagako's own doubts about pedantry, and have decided to delete some sections which were overly Buddhist influenced.

While it is not known when the text of *Sanuki no Suke Nikki* suffered the editing or miscopying which resulted in the many omissions and obscurities which mar all extant copies of the work, it is evident, from the colophon to the *Gunsho ruijū* manuscript of 1639, that the text had been severely corrupted by that time. The colophon reads:

*Book I:*
> The above was copied by Anchūsho no Yasuhiro, and by Taijin no Kageaki from the manuscript borrowed from the Retired Emperor; and was checked over together with the Great Counsellor Tomofusa from the Seikanji. The omissions and miscopyings were innumerable, and further corrections are required.
>
>> 2nd day 12th month 1639.
>> Head Librarian of the Palace Library.

*Book II:*
> The above was copied by the sixth rank Senior Chamberlain, Minamoto no Toshiharu, from the manuscript belonging to the Government Archives, and was checked over together with the Iwakura Middle Captain.
>
>> 16th day 12th month 1639.
>> Head Librarian of the Palace Library.
>
> The above *Sanuki no Suke Nikki* was copied by Nasa Katsutaka, and checked against the copy belonging to Hyakka-an Munekata.

This same problem, of omissions and miscopying, was remarked on by Kamo no Suetaka, who made a copy of *Sanuki no Suke Nikki* in 1778, to which he appended the following:

> Ever since, some time ago, I saw a reference in *Tsurezuregusa* to the fact that the phrase 'Fure fure koyuki', spoken by Emperor Toba as a child, occurs in this journal, I have for many years wished to see the work. When recently I saw a copy of the work belonging to the learned Shōen, I then fully comprehended the happiness of the daughter of Sugawara no Takasue on being given a copy of *Genji Monogatari*. Although it was the sixth month, when it is hot and the sun beats down, I forthwith made a copy of the work, wiping away my perspiration the while. In places where the meaning was confused, I made notes in the margin in *kanji*. Furthermore, in passages I felt to be erroneous, I with some trepidation recorded my own suggestions. There are still many places as vague as the autumn moon. They will have to await further study.

There are believed to be thirty-one manuscript copies of *Sanuki no Suke Nikki* in existence today. The existence of two, one said to be in the possession of the Kanshūji and the other said to have once belonged to the Mito Shōkōkan, has not been verified. The remainder fall into three categories:—

7

1. Those consisting of Book One only—
    (i) The Imai Jikan manuscript in the Mite Collection.
    (ii) The copy of the Imai Jikan manuscript in the Yamaguchi Prefectural Library.
    (iii) The manuscript incorporated in the *Zoku fusōshūyōshū* in the Mito Shōkōkan.
    (iv) The Nabeshima family manuscript held by the Yūtoku Inari Shrine.
    (v) The copy of the Nabeshima family manuscript held by Kyoto University Library.
    (vi) The manuscript in one volume in the Momozono Collection (I).
    (vii) The manuscript in one volume in the Momozono Collection (II).
    (viii) The manuscript in the Kansai University Library.
    (ix) The manuscript held by Imakōji Kakuzui.

2. Those consisting of Books One and Two, and based on the manuscript prepared by the Head Librarian of the Palace Library—
    (x) The *Gunsho ruijū* manuscript.
    (xi) The manuscript in Kyūshū University Library.
    (xii) The *Hasshū bunsō* manuscript in the Mito Shōkōkan.
    (xiii) The *Hasshū bunsō* manuscript in the Archives of the Imperial Household (Kunaichō Shoryōbu).
    (xiv) The manuscript formerly held by Murata Harumi, now in the Tenri Library.
    (xv) The manuscript formerly held by the Oshikōji family, now in the Tōdai Shiryō Hensanjo.
    (xvi) The manuscript in the Tawa Collection.
    (xvii) The Iwase Collection manuscript in the Nishio Municipal Library.
    (xviii) The Kinshidō manuscript in the Ise Shrine Collection.
    (xix) The Mifusho manuscript in the Ise Shrine Collection.
    (xx) The *Kiyokinagisa no shū* manuscript in the Ise Shrine Collection.

(xxi) The manuscript in two volumes in the Momozono Collection (III).

(xxii) The manuscript in the Sumiyoshi Collection.

(xxiii) The manuscript formerly held by Inoue Yorikuni, now in the Jinshū Collection at the Mukyūkai Library.

(xxiv) The manuscript formerly in the Nanki Collection, now in the Tokyo University Library.

(xxv) The Kamo no Suetaka manuscript held by Hagino Yoshiyuki.

(xxvi) The Kamo no Suetaka manuscript in the Kasendō Collection.

(xxvii) The *Zappitsu* manuscript in the Jinshū Collection at the Mukyūkai Library.

3. Those consisting of Books One and Two and based on the Kajima Shrine manuscript of 1648—

(xxviii) The copy of the Kajima Shrine manuscript held by Takahashi Tei'ichi.

(xxix) The manuscript in the Kansai Gakuin Library.

The manuscripts in groups 1 and 3, and the two *Hasshū bunsō* manuscripts in group 2, have no colophon, while the remainder have all, or part of the *Gunsho ruijū* manuscript colophon.[2]

*Sanuki no Suke Nikki* belongs to a genre known as *nikki bungaku*, or diaries with literary merit. The other surviving Heian period examples of the genre are *Tosa Nikki*, *Kagerō Nikki*, *Izumi Shikibu Nikki*, *Murasaki Shikibu Nikki*, *Sarashina Nikki*, *Takamura Nikki*, *Heichū Nikki*, *Takamitsu Nikki* and *Zaigo Chūjō no Nikki*.[3] Of these, the last four are more commonly regarded as belonging to the *uta monogatari* (poem tale) genre.

The *nikki* genre is in many ways the most interesting of the literary genres of the Heian period, since many works included in it contain elements characteristic of other later-developing genres, and in this sense the *nikki* can be regarded as something of an experimental form. It is important to understand that during the Heian and Kamakura periods the term *nikki* did not necessarily have its present connotations of a diary, or personal day-by-day record of one's actions and thoughts. The earliest *nikki*, in fact, seem to have been public rather than private works.[4] The term *nikki* appears to have originated in China, where it was used to refer to (a) the records of the actions and words of princes—i.e., a record of some-body else's actions; and (b) the studies of scholars—i.e., a record of one's own actions.[5] Thus the five *Chinese Classics*, said to have been compiled by Confucius, were referred to as *Kōshi no Nikki Gyōseki*. The original meaning of the word then seems to have been a record of facts. The addition of dates was probably only of secondary importance, to lend verisimilitude to the account.[6]

The main spate of *nikki* in China did not appear until the Sung period. In Japan the oldest surviving work which appears to be a *nikki* is a fragment of only two months entered in a calendar of 746,[7] while the earliest appearance of the actual term *nikki* is an edict by Fujiwara no Fuyutsugu, dated 821.[8]

The main motivation for the compilation of *nikki* in Japan was provided by the introduction from China in the eighth century of a bureaucratic form of government. This necessitated the keeping of records of all aspects of public life. For example, the activities of the Emperor were recorded in the *tenjō nikki*, kept by the Chamberlains (*kurōdo*); the proceedings of the Great Council of State (*dajōkan*) were recorded in the *geki*; the proceedings of the Ministry of Central Affairs (*nakatsukasa shō*) were recorded in *naiki*; while even the Inner Palace Guards (*konoe*) and Imperial Police (*kebiishi*) kept records of their activities. These records were made with the aim of providing material for the compilers of the national histories, based on the Chinese dynastic histories.

Many government officials, in addition, kept their own personal records of court and government proceedings. These, like the official records, were written in Chinese, and are known as *kambun nikki*. The most well known are the *Shōyuki*, written by Fujiwara no Sanesuke, and covering the years 978–1032; the *Midō Kampaku Ki*, written by the Fujiwara Regent Michinaga, and covering the years 998–1021; the *Gonki*, written by Fujiwara no Yukinari, and covering the years 991–1017; the *Chōshūki*, written by Minamoto no Morotoki, and covering the years 1087–1136; and the *Chūyūki*, written by Fujiwara no Munetada, and covering the years 1087–1131.

These *kambun nikki* cannot, however, be classed as literature, for while the authors do comment on the weather, the scenery, their state of health and the worry this occasions them, and sometimes even include Japanese poems and prose passages in the Japanese syllabry (*kana*), these works are essentially an unadorned, often almost moment-by-moment, record of the author's daily life.[9]

In a slightly different category, but still in the tradition of un-adorned factual recording, were the records of poetry contests, *uta awase nikki*, both of Chinese poetry and later of Japanese poetry. The *Teiji-in uta Awase Nikki* of 913 is usually considered to be the earliest surviving record of a Japanese poetry contest.[10] The very inclusion of poetry in these records gave them some literary merit, and as time passed, a distinct literary consciousness came to be displayed. A preface and conclusion might be added, and sometimes the writer was mentioned.[11]

These *uta awase nikki* were very similar to the *shikashū* or private anthologies already mentioned, and it was often hard to distinguish between a chronologically arranged *shikashū*, the poems of which were interlarded with long explanatory prose passages (*kotobagaki*), and a poem tale (*uta monogatari*) or diary (*nikki*).[12] Ki no Tsurayuki launched the literary diary form, when he wrote the opening lines of *Tosa Nikki*: 'It is said that diaries are kept by men, but I shall see if a woman cannot also keep one.'[13]

An actual definition of the genre was given later by the authoress of *Kagerō Nikki*, who wrote: '. . . she had occasion to look at the old romances, and found them masses of the rankest fabrication. Perhaps, she said to herself, even the story of her own dreary life, set down in a journal, might be of interest . . .'. A little later in the same work, the authoress gives her own definition of a *nikki*—'though this is a journal in which I should set down only things that immediately concern me, the shock of the banishment was something very close to me, and I shall be forgiven, I hope, for treating it in such detail'.[14]

The feature all the *nikki* have in common is not so much that they present a day-by-day account of their author's actions and thoughts, but that they each concentrate on a theme of central importance in the author's life. Thus *Kagerō Nikki* concentrates on the relationship of the authoress with Fujiwara no Kaneie, *Izumi Shikibu Nikki* on the relationship of the authoress with Prince Atsumichi, and *Sanuki no Suke Nikki* on the relationship of the authoress with Emperor Horikawa.

Another feature shared by the *nikki* is their public, rather than private, nature. All are dotted with remarks addressed to the reader, while it is evident that both *nikki* and *shikashū* were circulated among interested readers, some apparently serving as copybooks for aspiring poets.[15] Not that such works were intended for general consumption. Rather they appear to have been written for the benefit of the writer and a small group of friends, and only gradually became known to a wider public.

Nagako herself obviously intended her diary to be read and circulated, for it contains many remarks addressed to the reader, more so proportionately than any other diary.[16] In Book One, with its taut and objective account of Horikawa's death, she chooses not to break the tension with descriptions of how people were feeling, but rather calls on the reader for a sympathetic understanding: 'Although the Emperor's condition had been deteriorating these last few days, you can imagine my grief now that I realised that this time the end must be near.'

She continues such appeals to the reader's imagination in Book Two, and at times seems to have been writing with a certain group of readers in mind, selecting her material on the basis of that group's taste or experience:

> I shall not describe the Great Festival of Thanksgiving, but I expect you will be able to imagine it. Everyone is familiar with the proceedings, so I shall not bother to record the details.

Having completed her work, Nagako decided to have a trial reading of it. She put much thought into the question of who should be the first to see her work. She felt that this person must possess three qualities—he or she must yearn after Emperor Horikawa as she herself did, must be well-disposed towards herself, and must wield some influence in society. She finally decided that Lady Hitachi fulfilled these requirements, and invited her to read her work.

Lady Hitachi seems to have been quite impressed, though whether she lived up to Nagako's expectations, and helped introduce the work to society at large, is not known. It is known, however, that by the following Kamakura period, *Sanuki no Suke Nikki* was enjoying some degree of popularity. As has been mentioned, it is listed in the Kamakura period literary catalogue, the *Honchō Shojaku Mokuroku*. It is also referred to in two studies on poetry, the *Waka Iroha Shū* and the *Yakumo Mishō*. In the former it is given as 'the *Horikawa-in no Nikki* written by Sanuki no Suke', while in the latter it is given as *Horikawa-in Nikki*, with the name Sanuki no Suke noted below.[17]

A more substantial knowledge of the work is revealed in *Ima Kagami*, in the chapter entitled *Tamazusa*. In this are to be found various anecdotes concerning Emperor Horikawa, and the chapter concludes, 'There is a detailed work describing this Emperor, which was written by an Assistant Attendant in the Palace Attendants' Office, who was apparently called Sanuki. I once heard someone read this work. Some of you must have read it also'.[18]

It is also referred to in the *Tsurezuregusa*, a collection of random notes written by Yoshida no Kaneyoshi (Kenkō) about 1340. He writes, on the subject of the word *koyuki*: 'I wonder if this expression dates back to antiquity. The Emperor Toba, as a boy, used *koyuki* to describe falling snow, as we know from the diary of Sanuki no Suke.'[19]

Within the very broad framework of the *nikki* genre there was ample room for experiment with different styles of writing, and some of the works included in the genre have been seen as the precursors of various genres which achieved widespread popularity at some later time. *Kagerō Nikki*, for instance, has been seen as the first autobiographical novel (*watakushi shōsetsu*),[20] while *Murasaki Shikibu Nikki*, with its annalistic form, has been likened to an historical tale (*rekishi monogatari*).[21] Part of it, in fact, has been incorporated almost wholesale into *Eiga Monogatari*, commonly regarded as the first of the historical tales.

*Sanuki no Suke Nikki* is similar to *Murasaki Shikibu Nikki*, in that both cover an area of historical significance,[22] and it is interesting to speculate on the extent of Nagako's historical awareness. She herself compares the scene at Toba's accession with scenes described in *Eiga Monogatari*, and there is a possibility that she may have seen her work carrying on from where the latter left off. *Eiga Monogatari* covers, in essentially annalistic fashion, events from the reign of Emperor Uda (887–897) to the time of Horikawa. The first thirty books, thought to be the work of Akazome Emon, wife of Ōe no Masahira, the father of Horikawa's tutor, conclude with the words: 'There will be many more stories to add to this tale. It must be left to those who read or hear of them to carry on recording them.'[23] The next seven books are thought to be by another lady-in-waiting, Dewa no ben, while the last three are by yet another, unknown, lady-in-waiting. It has been suggested, though not proved, that this person was Suō no naishi, with whom Nagako was acquainted and exchanged poetry.[24]

Since *Eiga Monogatari* closes in 1092, in the first half of Horikawa's reign, it is possible that Nagako herself saw fit to take up the invitation in Book 30, and to continue the record for those years with which she was acquainted. The two works are similar in subject matter, since despite its title, which can be translated as Tales of Splendour, *Eiga Monogatari* is more a treatise on death, reaching its climax with the almost technicolour description of the death of Fujiwara no Michinaga. *Sanuki no Suke Nikki*, with its stark and realistic description of Horikawa's last days, may have been intended as a deliberate contrast.

While the annalistic style of Book One of *Sanuki no Suke Nikki* bears comparison with that of *Eiga Monogatari*, the style of Book Two has more affinities with *Ōkagami*, generally regarded as being the second of the historical tales. In this work, simple chronological treatment has been rejected in favour of a more topical treatment, with the material grouped in a series of biographies. The anecdotal treatment, relying on the theatrical device of two raconteurs, lends the work a dramatic quality, and proves very effective in the delineation of character. The manner in which the character of the central figure, Michinaga, is built up through a series of anecdotes, is similar to the depiction of Horikawa in Book Two of *Sanuki no Suke Nikki*, and it is interesting to discover that in the early thirteenth century the *Ōkagami* itself was regarded as a *nikki*. A passage in a treatise on poetry, the *Mumyōshō*, states:

A person of old said, 'In respect to works written in *kana*, the *Kokinshū* should be used as a model when writing a preface to an anthology of poems. *As regards nikki, one should take a lesson from the Okagami*, and as for introductory passages to poetry, one should follow the example of the introductions to the poetry in *Ise Monogatari* and the *Gosenshū*. As for *monogatari*, there is nothing to surpass *Genji*.'[25]

However, while it is interesting to know that *Ōkagami* was once regarded as a *nikki*, and fascinating to speculate that *Sanuki no Suke Nikki*, in its use of both the annalistic and anecdotal methods of treatment, may have provided a transition between *Eiga Monogatari* and *Ōkagami*, the question will doubtless remain unproven.

*Sanuki no Suke Nikki* revolves around the Emperor Horikawa, seventy-third Emperor of Japan, who reigned for twenty-one years from 1086 to 1107, and whom the authoress Nagako served for eight years. Her account of time spent in his service provides virtually all that is known of this rather shadowy Heian ruler. Supplementary material must be gleaned from works such as the *Ima Kagami*, diaries written in Chinese, such as the *Chūyūki* by Fujiwara no Munetada, and collections of anecdotes (*setsuwa*).

Horikawa was born, the second son of Emperor Shirakawa, on the ninth day of the seventh month 1079, and named Prince Taruhito. His mother was Katako (Kenshi), the real daughter of the Minister of the Right, Minamoto no Akifusa, but the adopted daughter of the Regent, Fujiwara no Morozane. Taruhito's elder brother Prince Atsufumi, who had been born in 1074, had died at the tender age of four. The story is told that Shirakawa, in his anxiety to have a son, asked the priest Raigō from Miidera to pray for the birth of a son. When Prince Atsufumi was born, Shirakawa was so delighted that he told Raigō he could have anything he wished. Raigō promptly asked for permission to establish an ordination hall at Miidera. The possession of an ordination hall, however, had long been the sole prerogative of the Enryakuji on Mount Hiei. Shirakawa, afraid of the repercussions if he consented, offered Raigō anything else instead.

Raigō refused and fasted to death, but before he died he uttered a terrible curse that the young prince would die. When the prince did in fact die, his death was regarded as a result of the curse, and Shirakawa this time asked a priest from the Enryakuji to pray for the birth of a son, and was rewarded with the birth of Taruhito.[26] Nevertheless, Taruhito was not to escape altogether from the curse, and it is the spirit of the same malevolent Raigō who appears to him on his deathbed.[27]

The death of Atsufumi was not the only blow that Shirakawa was to suffer, for his beloved consort Katako died at the age of 28 when Taruhito was only six. Shirakawa was so distressed by this that he considered abdication, but the following year the Crown Prince, Shirakawa's half-brother Prince Sanehito, died of smallpox.

Shirakawa was now faced with a succession problem. His father, Emperor Go-Sanjō, had abdicated in 1072 after only four years in office, and while his motives have been the subject of considerable controversy, it seems most likely that his action was designed to preserve that independence of the imperial family from *sekkanke* domination which he, as the son of an imperial princess rather than a *sekkanke* daughter, had been fortunate enough to achieve.[28] He had been obliged to confirm as Crown Prince in 1069 his eldest son, the future Shirakawa, whose mother was the daughter of Fujiwara no Yoshinobu. Yoshinobu was a half-brother of the Regent Yorimichi, but bore him no love, and had supported Go-Sanjō's claims to the throne in opposition to Yorimichi's wishes. With the birth in 1071 of another son, Sanehito, to Motoko, daughter of Minamoto no Motohira, Go-Sanjō seems to have seen the opportunity for imperial independence which he was seeking. Accordingly he abdicated in favour of Shirakawa, designated the baby as Crown Prince, and later requested Shirakawa that another son, Prince Sukehito, born to Motoko after his abdication, be made Crown Prince after Sanehito.

With the death of Crown Prince Sanehito, Shirakawa was faced with the dilemma of whether to follow his father's wishes and appoint Sukehito, or appoint Taruhito, son of his beloved Katako, and now aged eight. He decided in favour of the latter, naming him Crown Prince and then abdicating, all on the same day (twenty-sixth day of the eleventh month 1086). Taruhito thus became Emperor Horikawa, but Shirakawa had succeeded in avoiding *sekkanke* domination, since Horikawa's mother Katako was only the adopted daughter of the Regent Morozane.

When Horikawa was thirteen, his aunt, Shirakawa's sister Atsuko, entered the Palace, and in 1093 was made Empress (*chūgū*). Needless to say, because of the great age difference, no children resulted from the marriage. In 1098, when Horikawa was twenty, Shishi, daughter of one of Shirakawa's close associates, Fujiwara no Sanesue, entered the Palace. On the sixteenth day of the first month 1103, when Horikawa was 25, she gave birth to a son, Prince Munehito, the future Emperor Toba, to the great joy of Shirakawa. The Retired Emperor's relief at the birth of this child can be deduced from a tale of the event recorded by Fujiwara no Yorinaga in his diary the *Taiki*, as the story was related to him by Toba himself.

> Tonight the retired sovereign's tale touched upon the events at the time of his birth. 'Before I was born the late Horikawa was ill, and the entire court centred its attention on Prince Sukehito [as his successor]. The late retired sovereign Shirakawa once lamented: "Although I had left my household [i.e. become a monk], I had neither taken the final vows nor accepted a priestly name. If anything should have befallen his Majesty, I would have re-ascended the throne. Furthermore, the empress [Atsuko] had no children, and since time was passing, the posthumously-titled empress [Shishi] became consort. When she became pregnant, I offered prayers to the goddess of the Kamo Shrine for the birth of a son. In a dream she appeared to me in the sleeve of a garment, but she did not speak. Again in another dream she said that the child would be a boy, and she said that a certain item should be taken from the beams. Surprised in my dream, I searched along the beams and found a silver dragon. This dragon has been preserved and I still have it today. Furthermore, the garment in which it was dreamed she appeared was enshrined as her god body, and it is now in the priest's residence. Even now I make offerings to it ..." Very soon I was born ... Thus, there were several strange occurrences. My birth was not [completely the result] of human effort.'[29]

Horikawa's own joy was short-lived, for Shishi died on the twenty-fifth day of the same month, and the baby prince was put in the care of Ben no sammi, wife of Fujiwara no Kinzane. Horikawa's grief on the occasion is expressed in the poem

> In spring
> The very haze
> Around the mountain
> Is a reminder of my beloved.[30]

No time was lost in filling the position of Crown Prince, which, with the exception of the day on which Horikawa had been so designated, had been vacant since the death of Prince Sanehito. The appointment of Munehito to the position on the seventeenth day of the eighth month 1103 indicates that Shirakawa was anxious to secure the imperial succession in his own line, an achievement he had despaired of in view of Horikawa's weak constitution and history of ill-health.

Hurst well sums up the significance of these foregoing events:

> With the birth of Munehito (the future emperor Toba) a rare situation in the history of the Japanese imperial house came about. Grandfather, father, and son served as ex-sovereign, emperor, and crown prince. More important, none of these positions was hampered by Sekkanke maternal relations, the imperial position was totally controlled by the imperial house. It was an occasion of imperial unity and independence almost unmatched in Japanese history.[31]

Yet Horikawa, the central figure of this imperial trio, left virtually no mark on the history of Japan. There is evidence that he enjoyed, and was actively involved in, the business of government. Fujiwara no Munetada writes in the *Chūyūki*:

> Now, he became Emperor at the age of eight. When he was nine, he could recite the *Book of Poetry* and the *Book of Historical Documents*. He was by nature compassionate, and the Buddhist law was engraved on his heart. He reigned for 21 years, reluctant to blame but quick to reward, dispensing benevolence and radiating kindness. He was of an even-tempered disposition, and did not reveal his likes and dislikes. From the princes and ministers of state down to all classes of men and women, each and every one was touched by his benevolence. He was like a Yao or a Shun. Now at this time it is like losing a father or mother. The sagacity of my lord was extremely high, and he was already expert in various paths of learning. His natural talent, particularly in the fields of laws, ordinances and regulations, and customs and ceremonies; and in the amusements of wind and string instruments, could not be put to shame by anything in ancient times. From the time he became Emperor as a child, and throughout his reign, as far as his will prevailed, justice predominated in the awarding of rank and position.[32]

A tale in the *Zoku Kojidan*, compiled in 1219, also eulogises him:

Emperor Horikawa was the wisest ruler of all times. In particular, he took an especial interest in the affairs of the realm. He had all applications for official positions brought to him, and would sit up late at night reading them closely, and in places inserting paper markers—this matter is to be investigated, this matter is to be looked into again, etcetera. He made these notes with his own hand, and gave them to the lord-in-waiting the following day. Although it was on the whole very difficult even for a matter which had been closely investigated by the Emperor to be carried into effect, he would re-examine the matter, and would then probably give instructions concerning it. This was exceedingly noble behaviour.[33]

However, Horikawa's performance of his administrative duties was increasingly curtailed by the deterioration of his health. The first reference by the *Chūyūki* to the illness which was to bring about the Emperor's death, at the age of 29, on the nineteenth day of the seventh month, 1109, appears in the sixth month of 1092, when Horikawa was 14.[34] Thereafter the illness recurred persistently, with the years 1100 and 1101 apparently the only free years. During this time, as seen in Yorinaga's tale above, there was an everpresent potential focus of unrest in the figure of Prince Sukehito, who was upset at the way in which he had been passed over in favour of Horikawa, and who, moreover, was supported by the powerful Murakami branch of the Minamoto family. At one time, Shirakawa even contemplated returning to the throne, since he had not yet taken the tonsure, but Munehito's birth obviated these worries. Nevertheless, Horikawa's ill-health caused frequent postponements of government business and ceremonies, and Shirakawa was at times obliged to deputise for his son.[35]

Horikawa was thus unable to leave an imprint on the political history of his country, and it is rather as a patron of the arts that he is remembered. He became the focus of a poetic circle, many of the members of which were Horikawa's own relatives, being descended from Minamoto no Morofusa. Among them were the brothers Kunizane, Masatoshi, Akinaka, and Akimasa; together with the respective sons of the two first, Akikuni and Akishige; as well as the brothers Moroyori and Morotoki. However, the group was certainly not a Minamoto enclave for among the other members were Fujiwara no Mototoshi, Fujiwara no Nakazane, Fujiwara no Akisue, Fujiwara no Kinzane, Fujiwara no Toshitada, and the poetesses Kii no naishi and Suō no naishi. The leader of the group seems to have been Horikawa's uncle Minamoto no Kunizane, who compiled the *Renjaku Hyakushu* as a tribute to Horikawa.[36] The group was responsible for the compilation of the *Horikawa-in Ontoki Hyakushu Waka*, a sequence of 100 poems written to detailed specifications by imperial command, and submitted some time between 1099 and 1104. Perhaps the poetic enterprise for which Horikawa is best remembered is the *Horikawa-in Ensho Awase* which he organised to while away the dreariness of the rainy intercalary fifth month of 1102. On the second day of the month, a group assembled at the Palace and a series of love proposal poems from the men and the replies of the women were read. This was repeated on the seventh day, when poems of resentment by the women and replies by the men were read.[37]

Horikawa himself was quite skilled at poetry, and nine of his poems appear in imperial anthologies from the *Kinyōshū* onwards. He was aided in the composition of poetry by a light-hearted spirit, a punning sense of humour which defies translation.

This wave of interest in poetry seems to have been stimulated by the arrival at Court in 1091 of Horikawa's Empress Atsuko, and faded after the untimely death of Horikawa in 1107.[38] During this period there were twenty-four court festivities at which poetry was composed,[39] whereas there is no record of a Palace poetry contest in the next seventeen years, up to the death of Fujiwara no Toshitada in 1123.[40] With the death of Minamoto no Kunizane four years after Horikawa in 1111, the group which had centred around Horikawa, and of which Kunizane had been the leader, broke up, and the members merged into other poetry circles. It appears that thereafter poetry centred on the salons of the aristocracy rather than on the Court.[41]

Perhaps even better known than Horikawa's interest in poetry was his love of music. His favourite instrument was the flute, and in *Sanuki no Suke Nikki* Nagako describes seeing the remains of his flute music on the Palace walls, where he had pasted it, in the hope that by constantly seeing it, he would learn it sooner. The *Ima Kagami* tells of how the flautists among the courtiers revered him as their teacher, and after his death cherished the books he had given them. Among these flautists, his especial favourite was Tokimoto. In hot weather Horikawa would give him ice specially brought from the Palace kitchen, or if this was unavailable, would hand him a fan. There is even a story that the Imperial Guards of the Emperor's Private Office on the night-watch would challenge each other loudly or softly in harmony with his flute playing.[42]

Another story concerning Horikawa's love of music is as follows:

> Ages ago once again, in the reign of Emperor Horikawa, priests from Nara were summoned to the Palace to take part in the ceremony of reading the *Daihannyakyō*, and among them went Myōsen. During the reading, the Emperor played the flute in various different modes. Myōsen dropped to his knees, and presented himself in the garden. At the Emperor's command, he went and sat on the verandah.
> 'Do you play the flute?' enquired the Emperor.
> 'I play after a fashion', replied Myōsen.
> 'I thought as much', said the Emperor. He gave Myōsen his own flute to play and when the priest played the tune 'Ten Thousand Years' with indescribable skill, he was delighted, and without further ado, presented him with the flute.[43]

Horikawa was a devout believer in Buddhism. He went to considerable pains to be able to recite by heart the first two books of the *Hokekyō* or *Lotus Sutra*, and also made a copy himself of the *Daihannyakyō*, which sets forth the doctrine of perfect wisdom. At his request the Sonshōji was built, and dedicated in 1102.

This picture of Horikawa is corroborated in *Sanuki no Suke Nikki*, where he appears as a very likable person. He is seen at his best in Book Two, where his fun-loving spirit and tremendous enthusiasm in everything happening around him are illustrated by his organisation of a game for the ladies-in-waiting, and his personal arrangement of their sleeve-openings at the Chrysanthemum Festival. His consideration for others is emphasised by the three references to the occasion when he shielded the authoress from the eyes of the Regent by bending up his knees. Yet Nagako is careful to give a balanced picture, and does not hold Horikawa up as a paragon of virtue.

There are occasions when his impish nature seems to border on the indiscreet, as when he sticks out his tongue and flees on hearing that the Regent is to assist at his meal; and he is seen having a distinct fit of pique on discovering one evening that Nagako is anxious to leave for home. This tendency to give way to his emotions is more pronounced in Book One, when he is weakened by illness, and his feelings of self-pity lead him to believe that nobody is concerned about him. However, even during this period of crisis, there are flashes of his former gay self, as when he has the noblemen given large lumps of ice to eat, and he strives to the end to maintain his sense of dignity, refusing support from his attendants, struggling to dress himself, and joining in the reading of the sutras.

Nagako's account might be suspected of bias, because of her very intimate relationship with the Emperor, yet her picture of a monarch who inspired great devotion in those around him is corroborated by a tale found in Fujiwara no Yorinaga's *Taiki*. In an entry for 1143, Yorinaga records a conversation with the Provisional Major Counsellor, Fujiwara no Munesuke. Munesuke relates:

> There was a member of Emperor Horikawa's bodyguard by the name of Sadakuni. After Horikawa's death, he pined after the Emperor, and was always coming to my home to talk about events which had happened during the Emperor's lifetime. On one occasion he said, 'The Emperor has become a Dragon King and lives in the Northern Sea. I think I too will go there'. Some time afterwards Sadakuni sent his son Sadaaki to my home with a letter. It read, 'As I mentioned before, I am leaving for Lord Horikawa's dwelling place. If I perchance meet him, I shall tell him that you are always yearning for him. As I have always wished that Sadaaki, who brings this letter to you, should become a member of the imperial bodyguard, I beg you to look after his interests'. I could not refrain from weeping. Then, when I inquired into the matter, Sadaaki told me, 'My father Sadakuni went down to the province of Mimasaka, and became a monk there. He spent a year building himself a dragon-prowed boat. He then embarked in it, set sail, and after waiting for a gusty southerly wind, sped away towards the north. We have designated that day a day for purification and fasting'.[44]

Horikawa's ability to get on with those around him served him well in his relationships with both his father and the Regents Morozane and Moromichi.[45] Herein lay the possibility for those antagonisms which were later to rend the imperial and *sekkanke* families, and erupt into open violence with the Hōgen disturbance of 1156. However, Horikawa was fortunate, both in the calibre of the men with whom he worked, and in his own temperament, which, while never permitting him to become a mere political cipher, helped him to maintain the Confucian Golden Mean. Shirakawa took seriously the upbringing and education of his frail son, but otherwise seems to have been content to spend the first fifteen years of his retirement fairly quietly, devoting himself to his personal and family interests.[46]

This belies the impression often derived from his long tenure of office—as Emperor from 1072 to 1086, and as Retired Emperor until his death in 1129—that he was possessed of dictatorial ambitions. In reality, Shirakawa's long dominance of the political scene probably was due more to circumstance than to design. For while the imperial family had its troubles with Horikawa's ill-health and longtime failure to produce an heir, the *sekkanke* too was beset by a series of misfortunes which weakened its power at court.

Ill-health in 1094 had led Morozane to bequeath his positions as family head and Regent to his promising son, Moromichi, who unfortunately predeceased his father. On Morozane's death in 1101, *sekkanke* leadership passed to Moromichi's son Tadazane, then a mere 24 years of age. Because of his youth and inexperience he was not made Regent until four years later, during which time he was outranked by the Minister of the Left, Minamoto no Toshifusa. In view of Horikawa's ill-health, Tadazane's inexperience, and the fact that the Crown Prince was a mere baby, it is no wonder that in the final years of Horikawa's life, Shirakawa came to be regarded as the elder statesman of the Kyoto court. That this was a role thrust upon him is instanced by the events immediately following Horikawa's death. Horikawa died about eight o'clock on the morning of the nineteenth day, but it was not until about 1 p.m. that the Regent, after consulting with the Minister of Popular Affairs, Minamoto no Toshiaki, decided that Shirakawa must be informed of his son's death. Toshiaki was despatched on this mission, with instructions to find out what should be done about the succession and transfer of the imperial regalia. Shirakawa was naturally too distraught by the news to be concerned about the regalia, and Tadazane refused to make a move before receiving instructions from the Retired Emperor. It was not until the late afternoon that Toshiaki returned with an order from the Retired Emperor (*inzen*) confirming Munehito as Emperor, and appointing Tadazane as *sesshō*. In the meantime, Fujiwara no Munetada had become very fretful, informing Tadazane that the realm was a precious jewel, that the position of Emperor must not be left vacant, and that always in the past immediate action had been taken to transfer the imperial regalia.[47]

Inevitably, however, many courtiers felt that the *sekkanke* was the object of deliberate discrimination by the imperial house. Such doubts may have been justified at the time of Emperor Go-Sanjō, for he was most concerned to be free of *sekkanke* domination, and had tended to favour the Minamoto family. Apart from his previously mentioned marriage ties with the Minamoto, he had made an opening for the Murakami branch of the family in particular when he appointed Minamoto no Morofusa as Minister of the Right. The latter's sons Toshifusa and Akifusa later held the posts of Minister of the Left and Minister of the Right respectively, while Akifusa's son Masazane is the Minister of the Centre who appears in *Sanuki no Suke Nikki*. Through the marriage of Akifusa's daughter Katako to Shirakawa, and the subsequent birth of Horikawa, the family came to be well placed as maternal relatives of the imperial family, though that position was still nominally held by the *sekkanke*, into which Katako had been adopted.

Fujiwara no Munetada had complained of the changed situation as early as 1093:

> Up to now there has never been a case in which the Minamoto family held at the same time the posts of Minister of the Left and Minister of the Right, Major Captain of the Inner Palace Guards of the Left and Major Captain of the Inner Palace Guards of the Right. This year there have frequently been strange happenings at the Kasuga Shrine, and the priests of the Kōfukuji have revolted. Perhaps this was a warning? In addition, of the five Major Counsellors, three are Minamoto; of the six Captains of the Outer Palace Guards, five are Minamoto; and of the seven Controllers, four are Minamoto. This is in truth a rare achievement for another family, and is a great threat to the Fujiwara family.[48]

Again in 1102 he complained:

In recent times there have been 24 court nobles, and members of the Minamoto family comprise over half of these. There has never been anything like this before, but it must be the will of heaven.[49]

At the time of Horikawa's death in 1109, the Fujiwara and Minamoto families held twelve positions each, seven of which belonged to the Murakami Genji. Their feelings as they hover around their dying kinsman are easy to imagine, for his death was the first stage in the waning of their power. Some pinned their hopes on a restoration of Prince Sukehito's rights, and there was some fear of a reprisal from Sukehito and his supporters at the time of Toba's accession. The young Emperor's procession was secretly accompanied on that occasion by the warriors Yoshiie and Yoshitsuna, members of the Seiwa branch of the Minamoto family, on which Shirakawa increasingly relied for police duties. However, events did not come to a head until 1113, when a note was thrown into the Palace of Toba's foster-mother, Princess Yoshiko (Reishi), revealing a conspiracy against the Emperor. The ringleaders were a priest, Ninkan, son of Minamoto no Toshifusa, and a young man named Senjumaru, who was associated with another of Toshifusa's sons, Shōkaku, head priest of the Daigoji. Toshifusa was head of the Minamoto family, had held the position of Minister of the Left for 30 years, and was widely respected in court circles. Shirakawa ordered an investigation of the affair, as a result of which the culprits were exiled, and Toshifusa and his sons Morotoki, Moroshige and Moroyori forbidden to attend Court. This prohibition was revoked a year later, but the Murakami political power was broken.

The appearance of Shirakawa's close associate, Fujiwara no Tamefusa, at the investigation indicates the Retired Emperor's interest in the affair, yet the extreme lenience with which Toshifusa's family was treated is hardly consistent with the picture of a dictator bent on eliminating opposing factions.[50] In the main, Shirakawa would appear to have been concerned solely with preserving the independence, not only of the imperial family, but of his line of it, and for a time the Murakami Genji, like the *sekkanke* before them, had come too dangerously close to thwarting that ambition.[51]

Nevertheless, there were those of his contemporaries who were convinced that Shirakawa was intent on instituting a new form of government, in which the abdicated sovereign would assume the commanding role. In 1093, in the opening years of Horikawa's reign, his tutor Ōe no Masafusa had predicted, 'The affairs of the realm will now probably all be run according to the pleasure of the Retired Emperor.'[52] Fujiwara no Munetada was the most outspoken critic. On Horikawa's death in 1107 he laments, 'Alas, this is a degenerate age, and the realm has been much disturbed. But can this be attributed to the faults of the Emperor alone? The trouble lies rather in the fact that there was a Retired Emperor, and the affairs of the realm were divided in two directions.'[53] Again, a year later, he comments 'Nowadays the might of the Retired Emperor equals that of the Emperor, and in my view the Retired Emperor is the sole arbiter of government.'[54] And in 1129, he is found lamenting, shortly before Shirakawa's death:

> After the death of Go-Sanjō, he administered the government of the realm for fifty-seven years, and conducted the conferment of court rank and the appointment of officials according to his own will and in disregard of the laws. There has not been a case like this in the past.[55]

Munetada's words reflect an attitude towards the imperial institution which was subsequently more fully expounded by the Chief Abbot of the Tendai sect, Jien, in his *Gukanshō*, probably written about 1220. In this work, which may have been written to dissuade Retired Emperor Go-Toba from embarking on the Shōkyū War of 1221, he criticises the role of retired sovereigns, and advocates the restoration of the Fujiwara to their historical role as assistants to the imperial family.[56] To Jien has been ascribed the origins of the concept, if not the actual term, *insei*, commonly rendered into English by the somewhat misleading phrase 'cloister government'.[57] Jien saw the successive *in* or Retired Emperors who held office during the century from 1086 to 1185 as consciously arrogating power to themselves. Thus he writes of the time of Horikawa:

> Shirakawa and Toba in their two terms had behaved as if the Great Palace of the reigning emperor did not exist, and about this, people who knew the

ancient practices lamented: It is the Great Palace of the reigning emperor which is the foundation of the business of state. In the generations of these past two it is abandoned, there is no disposition of state business.[58]

This concept of rule by Retired Emperors was elaborated in the *Jinnō Shōtōki*, written in 1339 by Kitabatake no Chikafusa. Here it was stated that documents issued by the Office of the Retired Emperor (*in no chō*) carried more weight than the orders of the actual emperor:

Although the land had been ruled by the Regents, the affairs of the realm had always been conducted by means of imperial orders [*senji*] or orders of the Great Council of State [*kambu*], but from this time [i.e. of Shirakawa], orders from the Retired Emperor [*inzen*] and orders from the Office of the Retired Emperor [*chō no onkudashibumi*] became more important, and the position of the reigning Emperor became purely nominal.[59]

The actual term *insei* to describe the concept of rule by a Retired Emperor was apparently not used until 1871, by Rai Sanyō in the *Nihon Gaishi*, but has thenceforth become a widely accepted term denoting a system of government in which all important decisions of state were made by the Retired Emperor, thus making a complete travesty of the position of the reigning Emperor and the system of government of which he was head, which had been established by the Taika Reform, and embodied in the Taihō Code of 702.

Recently, however, there has been a re-evaluation of the whole concept of *insei*, in the light of studies of the powerful and influential families of the day, commonly referred to as *kemmon* or *kemmon seika*. Such studies depict the history of medieval Japan as a series of struggles for supremacy between competing kinship blocs, of which the Yamato *uji* or imperial family was one.[60] *Insei* then appears not so much as a new political system, representing a break from the Taika system, 'but rather as an organizational attempt on the part of the imperial house to reassert its own control within the existing system'.[61]

Admittedly, the system as it existed around the time of Go-Sanjō was rather different from that envisaged by the propounders of the Taika Reform edict, since the growth of large tax-free estates (*shōen*), especially in the hands of the Fujiwara family, had nullified any claim for the Emperor to own all the land in the realm. Jien writes:

The reason why a Records Office was established for the first time in the Enkyū era (1069–1073) was that the Emperor had heard that the realm was imperilled by the unauthorized seizure of public land in all the provinces of the seven circuits. In other words, he made use of this Office, because he had heard how during Yorimichi's time, more and more land was becoming known as the Regent's proprietorship, and how the *shōen* were filling the provinces, making it difficult for the *zuryō* to perform their duties.[62]

With the increase in the size and complexity of these *shōen*, there arose the need for establishing an administrative apparatus to handle those problems that had hitherto been dealt with by the provincial governors appointed by the imperial government. As early as the Nara period, some high-ranking families had established administrative councils (*mandokoro*), presided over by the family head (*uji no chōja*). These were now expanded by the creation of a number of bureaus, such as the secretariat (*kurōdo dokoro*) and the retainers' office (*samurai dokoro*), which would be staffed by clients of the family, ranging from the *keishi* (who would also hold lower-ranking public positions) to the housemen (*kenin*), retainers (*samurai*) and servants. The various bureaus were headed by directors (*bettō*), and empowered to issue in the course of their business various documents, among which were orders (*kudashibumi*) and directives (*migyōsho*).[63]

Such a pattern was adopted by all the *kemmon*, by court officials, and even by officials of the fourth and fifth rank, so it is not surprising that the imperial family also should have its own house administration. Yet it is the Retired Emperor's private household office (*in no chō*); the clients who staffed it (*in no kinshin*)—usually referred to as the 'close associates', or more damningly 'henchmen' of the Retired Emperor; and the orders issued from this office (*kudashibumi* and *inzen*), that have contributed much to the concept of an alternate government headed by a Retired Emperor.

Detailed examinations of the orders issued by the *in no chō* have revealed that, until about the time of the Hōgen disturbance of 1156, these orders were concerned primarily with matters of *shōen* acquisition and administration, with the welfare of the imperial house as a whole being of paramount concern.[64] In *Sanuki no Suke Nikki* Nagako herself is the recipient of several *inzen*, which concern relatively minor matters such as her transfer to the court of Emperor Toba and her attendance at certain ceremonies. While Emperor Horikawa was apparently able to flout the Retired Emperor's wishes concerning Nagako's transfer, she herself is advised by the person on whom she depends for advice that she had best comply with the Retired Emperor's orders.[65]

A more vexed question is the role of the *in no kinshin*. Membership of this group has usually been ascribed to a motley variety of groups that had not achieved power under the *sekkanke*, and in particular to members of the provincial governor, or *zuryō* class, whose objections to *sekkanke* growth have already been noted.[66] Go-Sanjō's establishment in 1069 of a Records Office or *kirokujo* to investigate *shōen* documents is the work for which he is best known and which earned him the support of the *zuryō* class. His son Shirakawa also was aware of the advantages of *zuryō* support, and made them many concessions. In fact, of the seven new developments listed by Fujiwara no Munetada for Shirakawa's period as Emperor and Retired Emperor, five concern the *zuryō* class—the advancement of *zuryō* by making gifts to the Retired Emperor, the appointment of children of ten as *zuryō*, the development of the governorship of over thirty provinces into hereditary tenures, the monopoly of *zuryō* posts by certain families, and the appropriation by the *zuryō* of dues owing to certain temples, shrines and families.[67]

It is information such as this which has given rise to a certain amount of controversy over the role of the *zuryō*, some seeing the Retired Emperor as being just as much a puppet in their hands as the Emperor had formerly been in the hands of the *sekkanke*; others seeing him as a despot, aware of the necessity of freeing himself from laws and traditions and using the *kinshin* for these ends.[68] Such a view is typified by the *Gukanshō*:

> From the time of Retired Emperor Shirakawa, the government was run according to the whim of the Retired Emperor, and the Regent no longer stood at its head. Among the first of Retired Emperor Shirakawa's close associates [*kinshin*] to benefit from this was Toshiaki. Later men such as Akitaka and Akiyori appeared. Unfortunately the actual Regents remained diffident, afraid of being pushed out of office by these conceited and low-born men.[69]

A detailed examination of the *in no kinshin* has established that by and large they came from seven families which had a hereditary clientage relationship with the imperial family as a whole, that virtually all had served at some time as *zuryō*, and that they tended to be appointed to posts in the capital where they could further the interests of the imperial house.[70]

The wealth of the *zuryō* was proverbial.[71] There are, for example, various anecdotes concerning Emperor Horikawa's tutor, Ōe no Masafusa. This scholar had held various provincial postings during his lifetime and was eulogised on his death in 1111: 'He was imperial tutor to three generations. He surpassed men in sagacity and learning, and outstripped everyone in literary ability.' Yet even he must have had his share of avarice, for the same writer continues, 'However, in a detailed examination of his character, there is a startling lack of integrity,' and states that five years elapsed before Masafusa proceeded to one of his provincial appointments.[72] An anecdote concerning Masafusa's return to the capital in 1102, having completed his term of office at the provincial government headquarters in Kyūshū, says:

> While he was returning to the capital with one ship filled with goods which had been taken legally, and another ship filled with goods which had been taken illegally, the legal ship sank, whereas the illegal ship arrived safely. Ōe no Masafusa said of this—'Life soon comes to an end. People should not be too honest.'[73]

The association between *in* and *zuryō* can probably best be summed up as one of mutual benefit. The traditionally wealthy *zuryō* could maintain the *in* in the luxury he desired, make contributions to the many temples constructed by the imperial family about this time, and help acquire official fiscal immunity for the *in*'s provincial estates. The *in* for his part could influence provincial postings, as well as making the appointments entitled him under the provincial allotment system (*bunkoku seido*).[74]

Of the *kinshin* mentioned above in the *Gukanshō* account, Minamoto no Toshiaki, who appears in *Sanuki no Suke Nikki* as the Minister of Popular Affairs, began his career under Go-Sanjō, and was appointed a Director of Shirakawa's *in no chō* in 1087. He was an Imperial Adviser (*sangi*) by the age of thirty-two, and on his death in 1114 he held the position of Major Counsellor. This success story has been attributed to the fact that in 1061 he had been appointed Governor of Kaga, and had served a double term there, during which time he had been able to establish the sphere of influence which had made him attractive in the eyes of the Retired Emperor.[75]

The Akitaka referred to appears in *Sanuki no Suke Nikki* as the Assistant Captain of the Outer Palace Guards (*emon no suke*). His father, Fujiwara no Tamefusa, who also appears as the Director of the Palace Treasury (*ōkura no kami*), was one of Shirakawa's most powerful associates. Because of the way Akitaka conferred with Shirakawa at night, he was known as the Night Regent (*yoru no kampaku*). It was said of him: 'The government of the realm rests upon a single utterance of this man. His power shakes the firmament, his riches fill the four seas. There is nobody, high-ranking or low-ranking who does not bow the head to him.'[76] His wife was the Ben no suke who appears in *Sanuki no Suke Nikki* as a nurse of Emperor Toba, and his son Akiyori was one of Toba's *inshi*.

The role of the womenfolk of *kinshin* families must not be over-looked, for while the *kinshin* never came to dominate the imperial family through their womenfolk as the *sekkanke* had done pre-viously, nevertheless many such families did form marital connec-tions with the imperial house, or form close relationships through the appointment of their members as wet nurses (*menoto*) to imperial children. A bright future was usually assured for any *kinshin* child which had the good fortune to be thus a 'breast brother' to an Emperor.[77]

Emperor Horikawa had four such nurses, though this was in fact unusual, since it was customary to have only two or three. The four were Nagako's elder sister Tōzammi Kaneko, Daini no sammi Ieko, Ōidono no sammi Motoko, and Ben no sammi Mitsuko. Of these, Ōidono no sammi, the wife of the Minister of the Centre, Minamoto no Masazane, and Ben no sammi, the wife of the Major Counsellor, Fujiwara no Kinzane, had the most successful careers. The former's son Akimichi was Provisional Middle Counsellor at the time of Horikawa's death, while the latter's sons Michisue and Saneyoshi rose to the positions of Provisional Middle Counsellor and Minister of the Left respectively. Of her daughters, Saneko, who appears in *Sanuki no Suke Nikki* as Dainagon no suke, wife of the former Governor of Aki, was one of Toba's nurses, while Tamako (Shōshi) became Toba's Consort Taikenmonin, and mother of the future Emperors Sutoku and Go-Shirakawa. Ben no sammi also happened to be the sister of Fujiwara no Tamefusa, previously mentioned as one of Shirakawa's closest associates. This liaison between Tamefusa's branch of the Fujiwara family and Kinzane's branch is illustrative of another tendency of *kinshin* families—that of forming a closely-knit group through inter-marriage.[78]

There was always a danger, of course, that these *kinshin* families might grow too strong, and this did in fact happen at a later date when the Ise Taira were able to install a child born to one of their members as the Emperor Antoku in 1180. However, at the time of *Sanuki no Suke Nikki* the imperial family was in a very strong position, and in such a court-centred work there was no room for mention of potential sources of danger such as the growing warrior power in the provinces, or the troublesome descents on the capital by armed priests, disturbed at the infringements of their temples' provincial estates by provincial governors, who were often in close association with the court. There had been a prophetical writing on the Palace wall in 1102 that the Buddhist Law would be destroyed by fire, and imperial dominance ended by force of arms,[79] but if one can draw any general feeling of the atmosphere of the times from *Sanuki no Suke Nikki*, it is one of optimism for the future. The description of the Regent Tadazane at a *kagura* performance, when 'it seemed that he was destined to prosper like the legendary two-leafed pine, which flourished for a thousand generations, and that this destiny would accompany him through the clouds into the next world',[80] gives no indication of Tadazane's later fall from favour and clash with his son Tadamichi, who was assisting him at this *kagura*.

Then again, the year 1052 had been heralded as marking the

beginning of the final stage of Buddhism, the Latter Days of the Law or *mappō*. In this final stage the Buddhist Law, having passed through the Stages of the True Law and the Reflected Law, would lose its power and mankind would enter on an age of decadence. However, at the time of Horikawa's death fifty-five years later, even though the beginnings of the decay of the old social system might have seemed to give some substance to the belief, Buddhism itself and the Buddhist monasteries were still very powerfully entrenched. The confidence of the clergy in the continuing role of Buddhism is reflected by Archbishop Zōyo, high priest of the Tendai sect, who prays over the dying Horikawa: 'I have served Buddha for many years, for over sixty years in all, and contrary to expectations, the Buddhist Law has not yet perished.'

While *Sanuki no Suke Nikki* contains little social comment and no social criticism, one of the chief attractions of the work is the candid description of Emperor Horikawa, who appears as a very real human being, complete with human foibles and weaknesses. At the same time that Nagako was writing her journal, Fujiwara no Munetada was expressing some very forthright views on the political scene—including the actions of the imperial family—in his *Chūyūki*. It would seem that in asserting itself as a *kemmon*, the imperial family of necessity shed some of the vague aura of mystery which had previously surrounded it, and laid itself more open to the sort of criticism that might be levelled at any *kemmon*. It was a fairly short road from Nagako's candour to Jien's notion of an alternative form of government headed by an ambitious *in*, and thus to the concept of *insei*.

The authoress of *Sanuki no Suke Nikki* is Fujiwara no Nagako (Chōshi), a somewhat elusive young woman, though probably no more so than most women writers of the Heian period.[81] She was the youngest daughter of the poet and minor bureaucrat Fujiwara no Akitsuna. Akitsuna himself was a grandson of Michitsuna, the son born to the former Regent Fujiwara no Kaneie by the authoress of the celebrated *Kagerō Nikki*. His father was the third rank Imperial Adviser Kanetsune, and his mother the poetess Ben no menoto. Akitsuna rose to upper fourth rank lower grade, and held the governorships of Tajima, Izumi, Tamba and Sanuki. He was also at one time a Director in Retired Emperor Go-Sanjō's *in no chō*.[82] In 1100 he became a monk, taking the name of the Sanuki Lay Priest, and the most probable date for his death is 1107.[83]

Nagako is not included in the genealogical work *Sompi Bummyaku*, which lists Akitsuna as having five children—Iemichi, Arisuke, Michitsune, Munetsuna and daughter Kaneko.[84] This could well have been because she was a child of his old age and was overlooked. It is not known definitely when she was born, but in *Sanuki no Suke Nikki* there is a passage in which the young Emperor Toba sees her for the first time and asks who she is. He is told that she is the child (*onmenotogo*) of Emperor Horikawa's nurse. An *onmenotogo* was the child who was reared at the same time as the child for whom its mother was wet nurse. Consequently it was regarded as the Emperor's foster or 'breast' brother or sister, and a close relationship existed between the two children. Nagako records that the young Emperor believed this explanation—and consequently of course was more inclined to accept her. While Nagako does not appear to have been an actual *onmenotogo*, the closest resemblance probably lay in her being born in the same year as Horikawa, in 1079.

Nothing is known of her childhood, or whether she accompanied her father on any of his provincial appointments. Like many girls of the time, she probably spent much time reading. In her work, she makes a fleeting and rather derogatory reference to old romances, but writes more approvingly of the historical tale *Eiga Monogatari*. Her writing is also embellished with various literary allusions, some to poems included in imperial anthologies, but others to poems which she apparently knew from the private anthologies which were circulated among aristocratic society.

The first recorded mention of Nagako is the occasion of her being made an Assistant Attendant (*naishi no suke*) on the last day of 1101.[85] She attended Emperor Horikawa in this capacity for six and a half years, but was probably at court prior to this appointment, since she states at the beginning of her work that she served Horikawa for eight years.

The position of Assistant Attendant was the second highest in the

Palace Attendants' Office (*naishi no tsukasa*), an office concerned primarily with serving the Emperor, but which also supervised Palace ceremonial and the lower Palace attendants. It comprised two Chief Attendants (*naishi no kami*), four Assistant Attendants (*naishi no suke*), four Junior Assistants (*naishi no jō*) plus two Provisional Junior Assistants, and 100 serving women (*nyoji, joju*).

The official duties of the Chief Attendants, who originally held lower fifth rank, were presenting petitions to the Emperor and transmitting his orders, together with supervising Palace ceremonial and servants. The Assistant Attendants, who originally held lower sixth rank, performed these same functions in the absence of their superiors, and were responsible for serving the Emperor's meals and for supervising the Sacred Treasures when the Emperor changed residence. The Junior Assistants, who originally held lower seventh rank, also participated in the serving of the Emperor's meals and the supervision of the Sacred Treasures. They also presented the Sacred Sword and Jewel at the accession ceremony.

Naturally enough, some members of the Palace Attendants' Office were singled out for imperial favours, and were raised to higher ranks. As early as the reign of Emperor Heizei (806–809), the Chief Attendant Fujiwara no Kusuko, who was a favourite of the Emperor, was raised to lower third rank, and the position subsequently came to be held by the daughters of Regents or Great Ministers. A Kamakura period work on Palace ceremonial and organisation, the *Kimpishō*, acknowledges that the Chief Attendants had become another category of concubine.[86] The same could have been said for the Assistant and Junior Attendants.[87]

The official demands made of Nagako in *Sanuki no Suke Nikki* are consistent with her duties as Assistant Attendant. During Emperor Horikawa's illness, it is she who is responsible for feeding him, and she is recalled to court after his death because there is supposedly no-one there of fifth rank to serve Emperor Toba his meals. Her participation in Toba's accession ceremony helping to raise the curtains around the throne, and in the *kagura* performance associated with the Great Festival of Thanksgiving, are due largely to her position as Assistant Attendant.

Yet it is apparent, if *Sanuki no Suke Nikki* is to be believed, that Nagako's relationship with Emperor Horikawa far exceeded the normal duties of an Assistant Attendant. The nature of this relationship, however, is difficult to determine. Nagako writes of remaining with the Emperor on nights when his Empress did not visit, but her treatment of this side of their relationship is very reserved. Occasionally the reserve is broken by the intrusion of some cherished memory, such as how they surveyed together the snow-covered Palace grounds early one morning before the rest of the Palace was astir, and a hint of passion is conveyed by a poetic allusion to the tear-drenched sleeves which once entwined her beloved. Generally, however, her emphasis is on those occasions when the Emperor singled her out for attention from among a group of ladies-in-waiting, such as the game of fan-lottery, or the display of sleeve openings at the Chrysanthemum Festival. At the latter, the Emperor insisted she remain, even though the colours of her outfit did not blend with those of the other ladies-in-waiting; while at the former, her display of temper, hurling an unwanted fan at the feet of the Emperor, is described by an onlooker as behaviour befitting a houseman or *ie no ko*. The use of this term is unusual, as it is one used later of vassalage, denoting someone with blood ties to his lord, though not of the lord's immediate family. On other occasions the Emperor is seen shielding her with his knees from the Regent, attempting to instruct her in Buddhist sutras and philosophy, and deliberately provoking her on an occasion when she wished to leave early for home.

Nagako is not officially listed among Horikawa's concubines—the respective daughters of Fujiwara no Sanesue, Prince Yasusuke, Fujiwara no Tokitsune,[88] and Fujiwara no Takamune. However, this does not necessarily exclude the possibility of her having been a concubine, since it was normal to record only the names of those who bore a son or who were of high birth.[89]

Nevertheless, Nagako's relationship with Emperor Horikawa often appears to be more that of brother and sister. She is in fact described by another court lady as the child of an Imperial Nurse (*onmenotogo*), a term which can be taken to mean the foster-brother or sister of the Emperor. Nagako herself refers frequently to the uniqueness of her position. There was nothing unique in an Assistant Attendant becoming an imperial concubine—the Assistant Attendant Muneko had borne Horikawa a son in 1103; but it would have been rare for an Assistant Attendant to be regarded as an imperial foster-sister, a position for which Nagako seems to have qualified by being adopted by her elder sister Kaneko, who was one of Emperor Horikawa's nurses.

On the whole, Nagako appears as rather a lonely figure, holding herself aloof from the other ladies-in-waiting. Her attitude is typified by her reaction to Horikawa's death:

> I just sat there beside the Emperor, pressing to my face the piece of Michinokuni paper, with which I had wiped away his perspiration. For years I had believed that my affection for the Emperor was no less than that of these people, but now I was haunted by the thought that my feelings must indeed be inferior, since I could not raise my voice in weeping as they were doing.

There is no real evidence that Nagako ever married,[90] and her family seems to have been concerned to establish her in court society where she might possibly find a patron or protector. Nagako records that she herself was most unwilling to go to court, but went to satisfy the wishes of her parents and elder sister.

This elder sister, Kaneko (Kenshi) had served at court for many years in the positions of Assistant Attendant and Imperial Nurse, and would be able to look after her much younger sister. Kaneko was probably Akitsuna's eldest child, and married his half-brother Atsuie. In 1079, aged thirty, she gave birth to a son Atsukane, and this was the occasion of her being selected as an Imperial Nurse to the future Emperor Horikawa, who was born in that same year. In 1086, when she was lower fifth rank upper grade, she helped raise the curtains at Horikawa's accession ceremony.[91] She was probably an Assistant Attendant at court for some time, since it was normal for Imperial Nurses to hold this position, but she is not actually referred to as such until 1088, when she is mentioned as being the imperial messenger from the capital to Yasoshima.[92] Probably as a reward for this service, she was elevated to third rank (*sammi*), by which title she appears when next mentioned in 1093.[93]

By 1101 she was known as Iyo no sammi,[94] a name obviously derived from her husband's position as Governor of Iyo. The appelation Iyo was probably added to distinguish her from her younger sister Nagako, who arrived at court about this time, and was known as Sanuki no suke, after her father's last provincial governorship. In *Sanuki no Suke Nikki*, Kaneko is referred to as Tōzammi, and her hysteria at Horikawa's death is very understandable in the light of the long and close association she had had with him. She became a nun the following month,[95] but did not die until 1133, at the advanced age of 84.[96]

Since Akitsuna had been a *bettō* in Go-Sanjō's *in no chō*, and his daughter Kaneko an imperial wet-nurse—an office closely associated at this time with *kinshin* families—it would seem that Akitsuna's family could be classed as a minor *kinshin* family. Further evidence of the family's cordial relationship with the imperial family is provided by the visit of Horikawa's Empress Atsuko to Akitsuna's house in 1094 to avoid a forbidden direction;[97] and the belief that Arisuke, Akitsuna's son by Go-Sanjō's favourite Jijū no naishi, was in fact the former Emperor's son.[98]

As Akitsuna became a monk in 1100, Nagako's appearance at court was probably a direct result of her father's wish to see his youngest daughter's future settled before his retirement. However, Horikawa's untimely death in 1107, together with the death the same year of her father Akitsuna and the retirement from the world of her sister Kaneko, left Nagako suddenly without her three chief supports.

It is against this background that one must view Retired Emperor Shirakawa's repeated attempts to persuade Nagako to return to court to attend the young Toba, then aged five. Shirakawa seems to have been motivated by a genuine concern for the welfare of this promising young member of one of the imperial house's client families.

Nagako herself seems to have realised by this time the necessity of having a protector, someone on whom she could depend for advice and presumably material support. When she receives Shirakawa's summons to attend court, she consults with the person on whom she usually relied for advice, who advises: 'It might be unfortunate for you in the long run, if you decline to go. You must look on this, my dear, as the working out of your destiny.'

Later, on arrival at the Palace, she is surprised to hear a child's voice singing. Then, suddenly realising that this must be the Emperor, she reflects: 'How absurd! If this is the master whom I am to regard as my lord and protector, I am certainly not filled with a sense of security.'

It would thus seem apparent that she had been urged to return to court to secure some sort of imperial protection. However, she seems to have retained doubts about the ability of the child Emperor to fulfil this capacity, and towards the end of *Sanuki no Suke Nikki* she seems to be transferring her hopes to the Regent, Fujiwara no Tadazane, much impressed by his personal success at the *kagura* performance:

> The sight of him, with his under-robes over his shoulder, made me think of the full moon rising over Mt Mikasa, and shedding its radiance down through the ages. I felt that he was in the prime of his life, just like the cherry tree in full bloom ... I decided henceforth to look upon him as my protector, for it seemed that he was destined to prosper like the legendary two-leafed pine, which flourished for a thousand generations, and that this destiny would accompany him through the clouds into the next world.

The event which precipitated Nagako's return to court was the need to find a substitute to raise the curtains around the throne at the accession of Emperor Toba, since Fujiwara no Saneko, who was to have performed the task, was unable to do so on account of the sudden death of her father, Fujiwara no Kinzane. Nagako, with very bad grace, acted as a replacement, but returned home immediately.[99] Persuaded to return to court again, she found herself developing a liking, almost against her will, for the child Emperor. Her descriptions of him dragging her off eagerly to show him around the Palace, asking to be lifted up so that he can watch a Buddhist ceremony over the top of a screen of state, and surprising her with his understanding of her love for his father, are quite unusual in Heian literature, where, apart from fleeting references in Sei Shōnagon's *Makura no Sōshi*, children are virtually ignored.[1]

Nagako acknowledges on several occasions that it is the young Emperor's childish vitality which brings her back to reality, for, from the moment she returned to the Palace, she was tormented by constant reminders of the late Emperor. It is possible to detect, in her obsession with the past, the seeds of the mental illness which has been suggested as the cause for her downfall from Court.

The last definite date in *Sanuki no Suke Nikki* is the last day of 1108, though the work was probably written in retrospect in 1109 or 1110. No more is heard of Nagako until 1119. Apparently from the autumn of the previous year she had been suffering some sort of mental illness. She claimed to have been visited by the spirit of the late Emperor Horikawa, and in his name spread around all sorts of stories. Emperor Toba, whose trust she had won, was inclined to believe these stories. The Retired Emperor, Shirakawa, therefore had her elder brother Michitsune, the former Governor of Izumi, summoned and informed that as his sister was suffering from some sort of indisposition, it was desirable that she did not attend court for a while.[2] The whole account is very unclear, but Nagako seems to have been predicting the birth of the prince who later became Emperor Sutoku. As there was some doubt as to whether Toba, or his grandfather Shirakawa, was the father of this prince, it may be that it was a matter of expediency that the indiscreet Nagako be removed from court before she revealed more, rather than anything to do with a mental illness.[3] Her outburst may in fact have been made in support of the Regent Tadazane, whom she seems to have cast in the role of her protector, and who at this time was out of favour with Shirakawa through his refusal for his own son Tadamichi to marry Tamako, who subsequently became Toba's Consort, and mother of Emperor Sutoku. If Nagako's fortunes were indeed linked to Tadazane's, she may have seen a revival of these fortunes after Shirakawa's death in 1129, but there is no further mention of her in historical records of the time.

While Akitsuna's family may first have come to the attention of the imperial family because of their provenance in the *zuryō* class, from which so many *kinshin* were drawn, much of the family's success must also have been due to its considerable literary talents.

In particular, the family was closely associated with the revival of interest in poetry which characterised the early *insei* period. Akitsuna himself is supposed to have received esoteric instruction in the art of poetry from his mother, and became a poet of some repute.[4] He left a *kashū*, a private anthology of 105 poems,[5] while twenty-five of his poems were included in imperial anthologies from the *Goshūishū* of 1086 onwards.[6] He is also supposed to have made a copy of the Hōjōji manuscript of the *Manyōshū*, thus contributing towards a wider knowledge of this then rare work.[7] He was much in demand at poetry competitions, and appears in those held at the Imperial Palace in 1078,[8] at the Kōyō-in in 1094,[9] at the home of the former Regent Fujiwara no Morozane also in 1094,[10] at the home of Fujiwara no Toshitada in 1104, and at a garden contest held at the Toba Palace.

Kaneko seems to have inherited her father's love of poetry. A poem by her is included in the *Senzaishū* of about 1188, and she was one of seven women who took part in the poetry contest held by the well-known poet Fujiwara no Toshitada in 1104.[11] Akitsuna's family seems to have constituted the mainstay of this contest.[12] A close relationship continued between the two families. In 1107 there is a record that Toshitada's house was burned down, and that at this time Iyo no sammi, the nurse of the late Emperor Horikawa, was living in his house.[13] As there is a note the previous year that Kaneko's home was burned down,[14] it seems likely that she had been living in Toshitada's house since that time. This relationship was cemented by a marriage between Toshitada and Kaneko's daughter, who bore him four sons, one of whom was the great poet Toshinari.[15]

Arisuke also inherited his father's interest in poetry,[16] and by his marriage to a daughter of Fujiwara no Michimune was allied to one of the foremost poetical families of the day.[17] Michimune's brother, Michitoshi, further cemented this relationship by adopting Sadamichi, one of Akitsuna's grandsons.

Nagako, however, does not seem to have inherited her father's poetic talents. The poems in her diary have little to commend them. She does not appear in the *Horikawa-in Ensho Awase*,[18] held in the rainy fifth month of 1102, nor in the poetry contest held by

Toshitada in 1104, in which seven women, including her sister Kaneko, took part. One of her poems is included in the *Shin Chokusenshū*.[19] This poem occurs in slightly different form in her diary, and it is conceivable that Toshitada's grandson Sadaie, the compiler of this anthology, may have felt sorry for this untalented member of the family, and have tried to improve one of her poems, so that he could include it. It is quite likely that Nagako was aware of these shortcomings, and consequently decided to prove herself in the developing field of prose writing.

The work that has come down to us serves as a memorial both to Emperor Horikawa and to herself, otherwise just two more of the myriad shadowy figures who flicker momentarily across the screen of Heian society, and then are lost in anonymity. Now this Emperor and his attendant, their personalities captured by Nagako's brush, and not too distorted by the tears of grief shed in the writing, will 'live on in people's minds and never be forgotten', just as Nagako wished.

# NOTES TO THE INTRODUCTION OF
## SANUKI NO SUKE NIKKI

1. *Honchō Shojaku Mokuroku* in *Gunsho ruijū* (1894), vol. XVIII, p. 998. This series will hereinafter be referred to as *GR*.
2. Imakōji Kakuzui and Mitani Sachiko (eds.), *Kōhon Sanuki no Suke Nikki* (1967), pp. 3–43.
3. *Tosa Nikki* was written by Ki no Tsurayuki under the guise of being a woman. It is essentially a travel diary, covering the period from the 21st day of the 12th month 934, when Tsurayuki, having completed his term as governor, set out by ship from Tosa province, to the 6th day of the 2nd month 935, when he arrived in the capital, Kyoto.

   *Kagerō Nikki* is a three-book work written by the daughter of Fujiwara no Tomoyasu. It covers the 21 years, from 954 to 974, of the authoress's marriage to Kaneie.

   *Izumi Shikibu Nikki* covers the relationship of the authoress, Izumi Shikibu, with Prince Atsumichi, from the 10th day of the 4th month 1003 to some time in the first month of 1004. The work consists largely of the poems they exchanged during this period.

   *Murasaki Shikibu Nikki* covers the years 1008 to 1010. It is in part an account of life at court, with especial attention paid to the births of the princes who later became Emperors Go-Ichijō and Go-Suzaku; and in part what appears to be a letter discussing Murasaki herself and other ladies-in-waiting.

   *Sarashina Nikki* is a one-book work by the daughter of Sugawara no Takasue. It covers the life of the authoress from 1020, when she was aged 13, to 1059.

   *Takamura Nikki*—also known as *Takamura Monogatari* and *Ono no Takamura shū*—consists of two virtually unconnected sections. The first deals with Takamura's love for his younger half-sister, and her death through their separation by the girl's mother; the second deals with Takamura's courtship and marriage of the daughter of the Minister of the Right, and his subsequent rise to glory. Takamura himself lived from 802 to 852, but the work is not by him.

   *Heichū Nikki*—also known as *Heichū Monogatari* and *Sadabumi Nikki*—is a work of 39 episodes, each centring around an exchange of poems, and each concerning Taira no Sadabumi. The work was written in the third person, probably between about 950 and 970.

*Takamitsu Nikki* or *Tō no Mine Shōshō Monogatari* centres around the retirement from the world in order to become a monk of Fujiwara no Takamitsu, eighth son of Fujiwara no Morosuke, and the sorrow caused to his family by this action.

*Zaigo Chūjō no Nikki*—also known as *Chūjō no shū*, *Zaigo ga Monogatari*, and most commonly as *Ise Monogatari*—is a work of 125 episodes centring around the life of Ariwara no Narihira. The author is unknown, but it seems to have been written about 950.

4. Tamai Kōsuke has gone to much trouble to give an accurate definition of the word *nikki*. In his work *Nikki bungaku gaisetsu* (hereinafter referred to as Tamai, *Nikki gaisetsu*), he examines Chinese *nikki*, gives 203 quotations from Japanese works, up to and including the Heian period, containing the word *nikki*, and concludes that the word meant 'a record of fact'. In a later publication, he again stresses this definition of *nikki*. See Tamai Kōsuke, *Nikki bungaku no kenkyū*. Hereinafter referred to as Tamai, *Nikki kenkyū*.

5. Tamai, *Nikki gaisetsu*, pp. 20-1.

6. Tamai, *Nikki kenkyū*, p. 74.

7. This is found among the works in the Shōsōin at Nara. See Oka Kazuo, *Genji monogatari no kisoteki kenkyū* (1955), p. 188.

8. This is found in the *Ruijū fusenshō*, a collection of edicts issued between 739 and 1093. See Tamai, *Nikki gaisetsu*, pp. 186, 188.

9. Imai Takuji, *Heian jidai nikki bungaku no kenkyū* (1957), pp. 526-8. Hereinafter referred to as Imai, *Nikki kenkyū*.

10. There is an earlier record, that of a contest held in the Ninna era (885-888) at the home of the Minister of Popular Affairs, but it is extremely simple.

11. For example, the record of a contest held at the Rohōdono in 1068 is concluded thus, 'I have recorded these things because I was instructed, "A *nikki* will be a suitable task for even a woman. Record these things before you forget them".' A final note is added, 'The *nikki* is said to have been written by Dewa no ben'. See *GR*, vol. VIII, p. 56. Other examples are to be found in Tamai, *Nikki kenkyū*, pp. 52-3.

12. The inter-relationships of these different genres has been the subject of much scholastic work by the late Ikeda Kikan. A concise summary of these theories is found in *Heian jidai bungaku gaisetsu* (1944), pp. 30-1. The relationship between *kashū*, *uta monogatari* and *nikki* in particular is discussed in 'Nihon bungaku shomoku kaisetsu 2: Heian jidai ge', *Iwanami kōza Nihon bungaku*, vol. XII.

13. Earl Miner (trans.), *Japanese Poetic Diaries* (1969), p. 59.

14. Edward Seidensticker (trans.), *The Gossamer Years: the Diary of a Noblewoman of Heian Japan* (1964), pp. 33 and 73.

15. The following passage occurs in the *kashū* appended to *Kagerō Nikki*:

    The memoirs of that garden party were borrowed from an attendant to the

Emperor's fourth son. The Empress died that year, and they were returned the following year with this poem written in the margin. . . .

See Edward Seidensticker (trans.), 'The *Kagerō Nikki*: Journal of a 10th Century Noblewoman', *Transactions of the Asiatic Society of Japan*, Third Series, vol. IV (June 1955), p. 221.

Another example of how *nikki* were borrowed is found in *Saga no Kayoi*, the second book of a now incomplete *nikki* written in the Kamakura period by Fujiwara no Masaari. In his work Masaari relates various literary evenings spent in the company of the nun Abutsu, authoress of *Izayoi Nikki*, the most well-known Kamakura *nikki*, and of her husband Tameie, son of the famous poet Fujiwara no Sadaie: '*Tosa Nikki, Murasaki Shikibu Nikki, Sarashina Nikki, Kagerō Nikki* and such works were sent to me from their place'. See Tamai Kōsuke, 'Kamakura jidai no nikki kikō', *Iwanami kōza Nihon bungaku*, vol. XII, pp. 46–54.

Other examples may be found in *Motosuke shū*, in *GR*, vol. IX, p. 648; *Ampō hōshi shū* in *GR*, vol. X, p. 35, and *Minamoto no Michinari shū* in *GR*, vol. IX, p. 699.

16. Imai, *Nikki kenkyū*, p. 202.

17. The *Waka Iroha shū* is a work in three books written by the priest Jōkaku around 1194–1196. *Yakumo Mishō* is a work in six books written by Emperor Juntoku (1210–1221).

18. *Ima Kagami*, Book 2, 'Tamazusa', in *Nihon bungaku taikei* (1926), vol. XII, p. 388.

19. Donald Keene (trans.), *Essays in Idleness: The Tsurezuregusa of Kenkō* (1967), p. 156. Hereinafter referred to as Keene, *Tsurezuregusa*.

20. Ikeda Kikan, *Monogatari bungaku*, in *Nihon bungaku kyoyō kōza* (1951), vol. VI, pp. 145–55.

21. Imai, *Nikki kenkyū*, p. 254.

22. Ibid., p. 257.

23. *Eiga Monogatari*, Book 30 in *Nihon koten bungaku taikei* (1964), vol. LXXVI, p. 338. This series will hereinafter be referred to as *NKBT*.

24. Mutsumura Hiroji, *Eiga Monogatari no kenkyū* (1956), pp. 593–600.

25. *Mumyōshō* in *GR*, vol. X, p. 755. This is a work in two books, dealing with Japanese poetry, and was written by Kamo no Chōmei some time after 1212. In *GR* it is entered under its variant title of *Mumyō Mishō*.

26. *Heike Monogatari*, Book 3, 'Raigō', in *NKBT*, vol. XXXII, pp. 225–7; and *Gukanshō*, Book 4 in *NKBT*, vol. LXXXVI, pp. 200–1 (hereinafter referred to as *Gukanshō*). The *Gukanshō* records events in the history of Japan from early times to the Jōkyū era (1219–1220). It was the first attempt to interpret as well as narrate history. The authorship is ascribed to the priest Jien, and the work is thought to have been written about 1220.

27. *Gukanshō*, Book 4, p. 204, and *Sanuki no Suke Nikki*, Section 13.

28. The term *sekkanke* is applied to that sublineage of the *hokke*, or northern branch, of the Fujiwara family which monopolised the two positions of *sessho* and *kampaku*, jointly referred to as *sekkan*.

For a discussion of the controversy surrounding Go-Sanjō's motives in abdicating see G. Cameron Hurst III, 'The Reign of Go-Sanjō and the Revival of Imperial Power', *Monumenta Nipponica*, vol. XXVII (1972), pp. 65–83.

29. *Taiki*, Kōji 1/5/16. Quoted in G. Cameron Hurst III, 'Insei, Abdicated Sovereigns in the Politics of Late Heian Japan, 1086–1185', (Ph.D. diss., Columbia University, 1972), pp. 160–261. Hereinafter referred to as Hurst, 'Insei'. Fujiwara no Yorinaga, the author of the *Taiki*, was the younger son of the Regent at the time of *Sanuki no Suke Nikki*, Fujiwara no Tadazane. He rose to be Minister of the Left.

30. *Zoku Kokinshū*, poem no. 1413.

31. G. Cameron Hurst III, 'The Development of the *Insei*: A Problem in Japanese History and Historiography' in John W. Hall and Jeffrey P. Mass (eds.), *Medieval Japan, Essays in Institutional History* (1974), p. 72. Hereinafter referred to as Hurst, 'Development'.

32. *Chūyūki*, Kajō 2/7/19 in *Shiryō taisei* (1934–44), vol. X, p. 231. This series will hereinafter be referred to as *ST*. The *Book of Poetry* and the *Book of Historical Documents* were two of the *Chinese Classics*, said to have been compiled by Confucius. Yao and Shun were legendary Chinese Emperors.

33. *Zoku Kojidan*, Book I, in *GR*, vol. XVIII, p. 694. The *Zoku Kojidan* is a collection of *setsuwa* in six books, compiled by an unknown author in 1219. The third book is now missing.

34. *Chūyūki*, Kanji 6/6/14 in *ST*, vol. VIII, p. 86.

35. Akagi Shizuko, 'Shirakawa-in to Horikawa tennō—insei shoki no in to tennō', *Shintōgaku*, no. 53 (May 1967), p. 30. Hereinafter referred to as Akagi, 'Shirakawa-in'.

36. Hashimoto Fumio, 'Minamoto no Kunizane to *Renjaku Hyakushu*—Horikawa-in kadan no shūen', *Shoryōbu kiyō*, vol. XII (Oct. 1960), p. 13. Hereinafter referred to as Hashimoto, 'Kunizane'.

37. *Uta Awase Shū*, 'Kodaihen', no. 21, in *NKBT*, vol. LXXIV, pp. 263–70.

38. Hashimoto Fumio, 'Inseiki kadan no ikkōsatsu—Fujiwara no Toshitada no shōgai wo megutte', *Shoryōbu kiyō*, vol. X (Oct. 1958), p. 6. Hereinafter referred to as Hashimoto, 'Inseiki'.

39. Hashimoto, 'Kunizane', pp. 8–9.

40. Hashimoto, 'Inseiki', p. 11.

41. Ibid., p. 21.

42. *Ima Kagami*, Book 2, 'Tamazusa', p. 385.

43. *Uji Shūi Monogatari*, Section 116 (Book 10, no. 3), 'Horikawa-in Myōsen ni fue fukasase tamō koto', in *NKBT*, vol. XXVII, pp. 285–6. The *Uji Shūi*

*Monogatari* is a collection of *setsuwa* compiled in the Kempō era (1213–1219) by an unknown author.

44. *Taiki*, Kōji 2/7/24. Quoted in Takeuchi Rizō, *Bushi no tōjō*, in *Nihon no rekishi* (1965), vol. VI, p. 317. Hereinafter referred to as Takeuchi, *Bushi*.

45. *Gukanshō*, Book 4, p. 204. For a detailed discussion of the relationship between Horikawa and his father, see Akagi, 'Shirakawa-in'.

46. Hurst, 'Insei', pp. 169–73.

47. *Chūyūki*, Kajō 2/7/19 in *ST*, vol. X, p. 231.

48. *Chūyūki*, Kanji 7/12/27 in *ST*, vol. VIII, p. 108.

49. *Chūyūki*, Kōwa 4/6/23 in *ST*, vol. IX, p. 193.

50. Apparently Fujiwara no Tamefusa made a personal appeal for a light sentence. See Takeuchi Rizō, *Bushi*, p. 182.

51. Hurst, 'Insei', p. 165.

52. *Gōki*, Kanji 7/6/16. Quoted in Takeuchi, *Bushi*, pp. 183–4.

53. *Chūyūki*, Kajō 2/7/19 in *ST*, vol. X, p. 231.

54. *Chūyūki*, Tennin 1/10/28 in *ST*, vol. X, p. 410.

55. *Chūyūki*, Daiji 4/7/7 in *ST*, vol. XIII, p. 65.

56. *Gukanshō*, Book 7, pp. 331–3.

57. For a more detailed discussion of the history of the term *insei*, see Hurst, 'Development', pp. 60–3, and Hurst, 'Insei', Chapter 1, pp. 2–9.

58. William R. Wilson (trans.), *Hōgen Monogatari, Tale of the Disorder of Hōgen* (1971), Appendix A, 'Extracts from the *Gukanshō*', p. 142.

59. *Jinnō Shōtōki* in *NKBT*, vol. LXXXVII, p. 142. The *Jinnō Shōtōki* was written in the autumn of 1339, when Japan was split between two contending courts. Kitabatake wrote this work in an attempt to prove the legitimacy of the southern court of the exiled Emperor Go-Daigo, of whom he was a loyal supporter.

60. John W. Hall, *Government and Local Power in Japan, 500–1700* (1966), pp. 118–20. It is generally agreed among Japanese scholars that the imperial family at this time consciously modelled itself on the organisation and actions of the *kemmon*, but there is some disagreement as to whether *insei* was an extension of the previous traditions of government or the founder of a new. One view is that, just as the Fujiwara political and economic power, while being a departure from the imperial system, was based on compensations legally acquired under this system, so *insei* too kept within the bounds of the old system and was not really a new departure. See Arimoto Minoru, 'Ōchō seiji no seisui', in *Nihon rekishi kōza*, vol. II, *Kodai—chūsei* (1964), p. 109. Another view, while agreeing that the Fujiwara always operated within the confines of the imperial system, is that *insei* was something completely outside this system, and can therefore be regarded as the first form of government by a powerful family or *kemmon* bloc. See Kuroda Toshio, 'Chūsei no kokka to tennō', in *Iwanami kōza Nihon rekishi*, vol. VI, *Chūsei*, vol. II (1963), pp. 279–80. The

Marxist historian, Ishimoda Shō, while acknowledging that the imperial family was developing the characteristics of a powerful family, sees *insei* as the last natural and inevitable outcome of the old imperial system. See Ishimoda Shō, *Kodai makki seijishi josetsu* (1964), pp. 357–9. Hereinafter referred to as Ishimoda, *Kodai*.

61. Hurst, 'Development', p. 63.
62. *Gukanshō*, Book 4, pp. 194–5.
63. For a fuller discussion of family house administrations see G. Cameron Hurst III, 'The Structure of the Heian Court: Some Thoughts on the Nature of "Familial Authority" in Heian Japan', in Hall and Mass, *Medieval Japan*, pp. 39–59.
64. Takeuchi Rizō, 'Insei no seiritsu', in *Iwanami kōza Nihon rekishi*, vol. IV, *Kodai*, vol. IV (1962), p. 103. Takeuchi draws his information from an unpublished thesis by Suzuki Shigeo: 'Insei-ki in no chō no kinō ni tsuite' (Tokyo University, 1961). This work has also been utilised by Hurst, who gives the best treatment in English of the subject. See Hurst, 'Insei', pp. 261–76.
65. *Sanuki no Suke Nikki*, Sections 25 and 26.
66. See note 62. For this view of *kinshin* membership see Ishimoda, *Kodai*, p. 363.
67. *Chūyūki*, Daiji 4/7/8 in *ST*, vol. XIII, p. 79.
68. For the 'puppet' view, see Hayashiya Tatsusaburō, *Kodai kokka no kaitai* (1955), p. 216. Hereinafter referred to as Hayashiya, *Kodai*. For the 'despot' view, see Ishimoda, *Kodai*, pp. 365–9.
69. *Gukanshō*, Book 7 in *NKBT*, vol. LXXXVI, p. 334.
70. Hurst, 'Insei', Chapter 8, pp. 277–99, and Hurst, 'Development', pp. 83–6. In the latter work Hurst restricts himself to seven *kinshin* families, while in the former he admits the possibility that there were more.
71. There was a saying—'If a *zuryō* falls, he will grasp up some dirt'. See *Konjaku Monogatari Shū*, vol. V, Book 28, Tale 38 in *NKBT*, vol. XXVI, pp. 116–19. There is also a song in the *Ryōjin Hisshō*, a collection of songs compiled by Emperor Go-Shirakawa (1155–1158), which runs: 'Deep in the mountains of yellow gold, A hermit's lad stood secretly, And heard the hare tell the tortoise, 'Our lord is becoming a *zuryō*'. See *Ryōjin Hisshō*, poem no. 320, in *NKBT*, vol. LXXIII, p. 401.
72. *Chūyūki*, Tenei 2/11/5 in *ST*, vol. XI, p. 96.
73. *Kokon Chomonjū*, Book 3 in *NKBT*, vol. LXXXIV, p. 110. The *Kokon Chomonjū* is a collection of *setsuwa* in 20 books, compiled by Tachibana no Narisue in 1254.
74. Hurst, 'Insei', Chapter 8. For a comprehensive list of imperial temple holdings, see Hurst, 'Insei', pp. 311–23.
75. Hayashiya, *Kodai*, p. 150.
76. *Chūyūki*, Daiji 4/1/15 in *ST*, vol. XIII, p. 14.

77. Wada Hidematsu, 'Rekishijō ni okeru menoto no seiryoku', *Kokugakuin zasshi*, vol. XVIII, no. 1 (1912). Hereinafter referred to as Wada, 'Menoto'.

78. Kōno Fusao, 'Shirakawa-in no kinshindan no ichikōsatsu', *Nihon rekishi*, no. 145 (July 1960), pp. 36–51.

79. *Chūyūki*, Kōwa 4/10/19 in *ST*, vol. IX, p. 223.

80. *Sanuki no Suke Nikki*, Section 49.

81. There were many years of confusion over the authorship of *Sanuki no Suke Nikki*. At one time, the authoress was thought to be Nijō-in no Sanuki, the daughter of Minamoto no Yorimasa, but this theory disregarded the fact that Yorimasa's daughter lived after the time of Emperor Horikawa. See Fujioka Sakutarō, *Kokubungaku zenshi: Heianchō hen* (1906), p. 550. In 1909 Sakurai Hideshi stated that the authoress was the nurse of Emperor Horikawa, Iyo no sammi Kaneko, the daughter of the Sanuki Lay Priest, Fujiwara no Akitsuna. See Sakurai Hideshi, 'Sanuki no suke kō', *Kokugakuin zasshi*, vol. XV, no. 7 (July 1909), pp. 36–7. This view was supported in 1927 by Ikeda Kikan. See Ikeda Kikan, *Kyūtei joryū nikki bungaku* (1965), pp. 159–65. However, as early as 1912, Wada Hidesmatsu had started to move in the right direction by stating that the authoress was Sanuki no suke Kaneko, the younger sister of Horikawa's nurse, Iyo no sammi. See Wada, 'Menoto', p. 42. In 1917 Sakurai Hideshi changed his views on the subject, and decided that the authoress was the younger sister of Iyo no sammi Kaneko. See Sakurai Hideshi, 'Sanuki no suke nikki sakusha ni tsuite', *Waka take*, (Feb. 1917). Referred to in Tamai Kōsuke, *Sanuki no suke nikki*, in *Nihon koten zensho* (1964), p. 18. Hereinafter referred to as Tamai, *Sanuki*. The confusion was ended finally by Tamai Kōsuke in 1929 in an authoritative article in which he proved conclusively that the authoress was in fact Nagako, the younger sister of Iyo no sammi Kaneko. See Tamai Kōsuke, 'Sanuki no suke nikki sakusha ni tsuite', *Shigaku zasshi*, vol. XL, no. 9 (Sept. 1929). Hereinafter referred to as Tamai, 'Sakusha'. This article was the result of much painstaking research through contemporary records written in Chinese, and the conclusions are indisputable.

82. Takeuchi, *Bushi*, p. 159.

83. The *Sompi Bummyaku*, a collection of genealogical tables of some of the most important families in Japan, compiled by Tōin Kinsada (1340–1399), gives the date of Akitsuna's death as 1103. However, these tables suffer from many omissions and inaccuracies, and the date given for Akitsuna's death has been questioned. Hagitani Boku has taken up the point that Akitsuna was present at the poetry contest held in 1104 at the home of Fujiwara no Toshitada, and consequently favours placing his death between the sixteenth day of the fourth month 1107, and the fifth day of the eighth month 1107. On the former date there is a mention of Akitsuna's grandson Atsukane accompanying the Regent to the Kamo Shrine. This, coupled with a reference in the *Chūyūki* to the household of Akitsuna, on the tenth day of the same month, would indicate

that Akitsuna was still alive at this time. On the latter date, Akitsuna is referred to as 'the late Akitsuna'. See 'Chōji gannen gogatsu nijū rokunichi sakone no gonchūjō Toshitada uta awase', *Heianchō uta awase taisei* (1961), vol. V, p. 1602. Hereinafter referred to as Hagitani.

84. Iemichi and Michitsune were the sons of the daughter of the Governor of Mino, Fujiwara no Takatsune. Iemichi rose to the same rank as his father and held the governorship of Kaga, while Michitsune rose to lower fifth rank upper grade, and held the governorship of Izumi. Iemichi died in 1116 aged 61. Arisuke was of more aristocratic descent, for his mother was Jijū no naishi, a daughter of Tsunekuni, and Arisuke was in fact said to be the son of Emperor Go-Sanjō. Arisuke rose to the same rank as his father, and held the governorships of Kai, Tosa, Kii and Ōmi. He died in 1131.

85. *Chūyūki*, Kōwa 4/1/1 in *ST*, vol. IX, p. 144.

86. *Kimpishō*, in *Shinshū kōgaku sōsho*, vol. V, p. 169. The *Kimpishō* was written about 1221 by Emperor Juntoku. It details Palace ceremonial, organisation etc.

87. For instance, Emperor Shirakawa had bestowed his attentions on the Assistant Attendant, Fujiwara no Tsuneko, while Emperor Go-Sanjō had favoured the Junior Assistant, Jijū no naishi, who was the mother of Nagako's half-brother Arisuke.

88. Fujiwara no Tokitsune was the younger half-brother of Nagako's father, Akitsuna, and consequently Nagako and Tokitsune's daughter were cousins. The child born to Tokitsune's daughter in 1104 was given the name Saiun.

89. Imai Gen'e, 'Sanuki no Suke Nikki', *Kokubungaku kaishaku to kanshō*, vol. XXVI, no. 2 (Feb. 1961), p. 74.

90. Tamai Kōsuke has proposed both Fujiwara no Toshitada and Fujiwara no Yasuzane as possible husbands for Nagako. Toshitada did in fact marry one of Kaneko's daughters, and Tamai suggests that, as it seems possible that Kaneko may have adopted her younger sister, Nagako may then have been the daughter in question. He first puts forward this theory in Tamai, 'Sakusha', p. 118, and develops it in 'Sanuki no suke nikkichū no jimbutsu', *Shigaku zasshi*, vol. XLI, no. 11 (Nov. 1930), pp. 93–5, and in Tamai, *Sanuki*, pp. 23–6. Tamai himself points out that the flaw in his argument is that the *Sompi Bummyaku* lists Toshitada's first four sons as having the same mother, the daughter of the governor of Iyo, Atsuie. This girl is described in the *Meigetsuki* as the younger sister of Atsukane. As Atsukane was 13 in 1091, when the first of Toshitada's four sons was born, this younger sister would have become a mother before she was 13, which is unlikely. However, Tamai overrides this difficulty by pointing to other mistakes in the *Sompi Bummyaku*, e.g., Atsuie's genealogical table gives Toshinari's mother as the daughter of Atsukane, while Toshitada's table gives her as the daughter of Atsuie. See Tamai, *Sanuki*, p. 24. Nevertheless Tamai's theories have found quite wide acceptance. For example, Ōtomo

Yōko, 'Sanuki no suke nikki sakusha kōshō-Fujiwara no Chōshi—Toshinari kyō no koto ni tsuite', *Joshi daikokubun*, vol. X (Oct. 1958).

Fujiwara no Yasuzane, who died in 1102, is proposed as Nagako's first husband. The basis for this argument is that, when considering returning to court, Nagako refers to a sorrow she has experienced in the past. The *Sompi Bummyaku* gives one of Yasuzane's wives, the mother of his sons Sanenobu and Sadamichi, as 'the daughter of Fujiwara no Akitsuna'; and in the *Kinyōshū* of about 1127 there is a poem by the mother of Sanenobu, lamenting her separation from Yasuzane. Tamai therefore suggests that Nagako was this unspecified daughter, and that the sorrow she refers to is her separation from Yasuzane and his subsequent death. See Tamai, *Sanuki*, pp. 27-8. However, as the younger of the two sons, Sadamichi, was born in 1085 or 1095, it seems unlikely that Nagako, then still a child, could have been the mother of both. Moreover, if Nagako had been married to either Yasuzane or Toshitada, it would have been more usual for her to have been referred to as such in the passage describing her dismissal from court, rather than as the daughter of Atkitsuna, who had been dead for some years. See Morita Kenkichi, 'Sanuki no suke nikki no seiritsu', *Kokugo kokubun*, vol. XXII, no. 1 (Jan. 1963).

91. *Tenso reiki shokushō roku*, in *GR*, vol. II, p. 308. Hereinafter referred to as *Tenso reiki*.

92. *Chūyūki*, Kanji 2/12/17 in *ST*, vol. VIII, p. 21. On the accession of a new Emperor, a propitious day was chosen, after the Great Festival of Thanksgiving, and a group of people would travel to Naniwa in the Province of Settsu to worship the gods, give thanks for the foundation of the country and pray for peaceful government. This was known as the *Yasoshima no matsuri*. One of the group who went there always held the position of Assistant Attendant.

93. *Chūyūki*, Kanji 7/2/22 in *ST*, vol. XIV, p. 255. Tamai points to a similar instance in Book I of *Heiji Monogatari*, where the wife of Nobunishi, Kii no sammi, a nurse to Emperor Go-Shirakawa, was raised to third rank as a reward for going to Yasoshima. See Tamai, 'Sakusha', p. 115.

94. *Denreki*, Kōwa 3/5/16 in *Dainihon kokiroku* (1960), Book I, p. 53. *Denreki* is the diary kept by Fujiwara no Tadazane, the Regent who appears in *Sanuki no Suke Nikki*. It covers the period 1098–1118.

95. *Chūyūki*, Kajō 2/8/5 in *ST*, vol. X, p. 242.

96. *Chūyūki*, Chōjō 2/7/14 in *ST*, vol. XIV, p. 54.

97. *Chūyūki*, Kanji 8/1/24 in *ST*, vol. VIII, p. 119.

98. *Sompi Bummyaku*, vol. I, in *Kokushi taikei*, vol. LVIII, p. 340, and *Ima Kagami*, Book 4, 'Fushimi no yuki no ashita', p. 431.

99. *Tenso reiki*, p. 308. However, *Chūyūki* (Kajo 2/12/1) records that the task was performed by her elder sister Kaneko. See *ST*, vol. X, p. 292. It was this error which caused the long years of confusion over the authorship of *Sanuki no Suke Nikki*.

1. Sei Shōnagon served as a lady-in-waiting to Empress Sadako in the last decade of the tenth century. Her *Pillow Book* (*Makura no Sōshi*) is the forerunner of the *zuihitsu* genre (occasional notes, random jottings), and has been described by Arthur Waley as 'the most important document of the period that we possess'.

2. *Chōshūki*, Gen'ei 2/8/23, in *ST*, vol. VI, pp. 158–9. The *Chōshūki* is the diary written in Chinese by Minamoto no Morotoki, and covers the years 1087–1136.

3. *Kojidan*, Book 2 in *Kokushi taikei* (1932), vol. XVIII, p. 40. The *Kojidan* is a collection of *setsuwa* in six books, written by Minamoto no Akikane, between 1212 and 1215. See also Hurst, 'Insei', pp. 184–7.

4. *Sandaishū no Aida no Koto*, in *GR*, vol. X, p. 607. The *Sandaishū no Aida no Koto* was written by the poet Fujiwara no Sadaie (Teika). In it he refers to Iyo no sammi Kaneko, Imperial Nurse to Emperor Horikawa, and states she was the maternal grandmother of his own father, Toshinari.

5. This was called variously *Akitsuna Ason Shū* or *Sanuki Nyūdō Shū*. See *GR*, vol. IX. The Imperial Household Library (*Zushoryō*) manuscript contains 105 poems, but the *GR* version has four less.

6. The *Chokusen Sakusha Bunrui* is a useful work compiled in the mid-fourteenth century, which lists poets whose works were included in imperial anthologies, together with a few biographical details. See Itō Yoshio *et al.* (eds.), *Waka bungaku daijiten* (1962).

7. *Fukuro Sōshi*, Book I, in *Zoku gunsho ruijū*, vol. XVI, part 2, p. 773.

8. *GR*, vol. XVIII, pp. 58–62.

9. *GR*, vol. XVIII, pp. 65–8.

10. *Uta Awase Shū*, 'Kodai hen', no. 19, in *NKBT*, vol. LXXIV, pp. 220–43.

11. Toshitada was a grandson of Fujiwara no Michinaga's son Nagaie. This Nagaie had been well-known as a poet, and the poetic tradition was kept alive in the family by his son Tadaie and grandson Toshitada. Toshitada's son, Toshinari, and grandson Sadaie (Teika) rank among the greatest of all Japanese poets. In 1188 Toshinari completed the compilation of the *Senzaishū*, and in 1201 was appointed with his son Sadaie as Secretary of the restored Bureau of Japanese Poetry. Sadaie helped in the compilation of the *Shin Kokinshū*, which was completed in 1206, and was solely responsible for the compilation of the *Shin Chokusenshū*, completed in 1234.

12. Sano Michi, 'Uta awase nidai-Tentoku uta awase, Toshitada ason ke uta awase', *Joshi daibungaku*, no. 8. Referred to in Hagitani, p. 1600.

13. *Chūyūki*, Kajō 2/9/17 in *ST*, vol. X, p. 260.

14. *Chūyūki*, Kajō 1/7/25 in *ST*, vol. X, p. 130.

15. In the *Meigetsuki*, (Shōji 2/10/11), also written by Sadaie, there is a statement that Sadaie's grandmother was the younger sister of Kaneko's son, Atsukane. See Tamai, 'Jimbutsu'.

16. A poem by Arisuke is included in the *Kinyōshū*, poem no. 645.

17. Michimune held various posts as provincial governor, and was a poet of some repute, having five poems included in imperial anthologies. He died in 1084. Michitoshi (1047–1099) rose to the position of Provisional Middle Councillor, and was in a fortunate position because his younger sister was a favourite of Emperor Shirakawa. He was commanded by Shirakawa to compile the *Goshūishū*, which was completed in 1086.

18. 'Horikawa-in Ensho Awase', in *NKBT*, vol. LXXIV, 'Kodai hen', no. 21, pp. 263–70.

19. *Shin Chokusenshū*, poem no. 1224. This corresponds to poem no. 18 in her diary.

# SANUKI NO SUKE NIKKI

# BOOK ONE

## Prologue

I    The sky this fifth month, overcast with the promise of further early summer rains, reflects my mood, and like the peasants out planting rice-seedlings, I will have difficulty drying the hem of my robe. How appropriate it all seems. This is a depressing season at the best of times, but here in the tranquil atmosphere of my home I am more prey than usual to the thoughts of happenings past and present which keep assailing me, and I am filled with sadness.[1]

When I look outside, the banked clouds and lowering sky seem to be in sympathy with me, and their leaden oppressive aspect makes me appreciate the imagery of the poet who wrote of 'the clouded vault'.[2] I feel my heart has clouded over with grief, and my tears are as the raindrops falling on the irises decorating the eaves.[3] Even the *hototogisu*, for whom the mountain of death is no barrier, joins its mourning cries with mine, and with the passing of each short summer night, I am haunted with memories of events now long past, and am unable to restrain my tears.[4]

When I think back on my time in the service of my lord—viewing the blossom in spring and the leaves in autumn, drinking in the brightness of a moonlit night, attending the Emperor on a snowy morning—I was never far from his side in the eight years I spent in his service.[5] And there was no lack of pleasant moments when the Emperor was about. The religious observances in the morning, the sound of the Emperor playing the flute in the evening —these are hard to forget.[6] It is in an attempt to console myself that I am writing down these various memories as they come to mind.[7]

However, my eyes are so blurred with tears, that I cannot see my brush-strokes, and as my tears fall and merge with the water on my inkstone, I realise that the very words I am writing will be so blurred as to be unreadable, and this provokes a fresh wave of tears. Although I took up my brush in the hope that writing might distract me from my sorrow, I am as inconsolable as those who gazed on Mount Obasute, and am quite unable to control my grief.[8]

**2** It was on the twentieth day of the sixth month that the Emperor seemed to be feeling out of sorts.[9] From time to time he would lie down.

'I should say that this is what people call an illness. Why is it that nobody pays it any attention?' he said.

He was evidently feeling sorry for himself, but now it is I who am sorry that—even though such matters were not mine to arrange—prayer ceremonies were not begun for his recovery, nor thought given to the possibility of an abdication—this was left to the very end—before the Emperor's illness became too serious.[10]

**3** Then, from the sixth day of the seventh month, the Emperor's illness took a turn for the worse. He could hardly have been said to be well for some months past, but he had never appeared to be suffering as he was now. And now that his illness had taken this turn, everyone was united by the common anxiety over what the outcome might be.

And just at this very time, the high-ranking ladies-in-waiting were prevented, for various reasons, from attending upon the Emperor. One was confined with child, one was in mourning for her mother, and yet another had retired from court some time ago, and had not attended court these past two or three years.[11] Of the Emperor's nurses, Tōzammi was absent from court, suffering from a fever, while Ben no sammi could not attend upon the Emperor as she would have wished, since she had been responsible for bringing up the Crown Prince after the death of his mother. Besides which, she too was at the moment suffering from the ague. So only Ōidono no sammi, Daini no sammi and myself—three in all—were in attendance.[12]

Such was the situation—and yet, since even when someone of low birth is suffering from illness, he requires constant attention, and it is best if he can be tended by a host of relatives, how much more desirable is such care in a case such as this.

4    As the day drew on, and the Emperor seemed to find the pain unbearable, a messenger was sent to report on his condition to Retired Emperor Shirakawa.[13]

'The Retired Emperor is shocked, and has moved forthwith to the Northern Palace, in order to make enquiries after the Emperor's health from close at hand,' the messenger reported back.[14]

The Emperor seemed to be in such pain, that I set about moving the tall oil-lamps closer to him than was the custom. Then suddenly the Emperor apparently stopped breathing altogether.

'Alas! How terrible!' everyone wept. Just then the Minister of the Centre and the Regent appeared, and began a vigil beside the Emperor.[15]

There was a general commotion and babbling of voices. Messengers were sent off to summon Archbishop Zōyo, and the Masters of Ascetism, Raiki and Zōken.[16] Raiki arrived forthwith, and began reading the sutras and earnestly invoking Buddha. After a little while, the Emperor made a slight movement, which provoked a fresh stir from those present.

'That will do no good now. Just transfer this evil spirit from me,' the Emperor said, on hearing the sutras being read.

Accordingly, a medium was sent for, and brought to the Emperor's bedside. You can imagine how awful it was as the evil spirit was transferred! The medium, into whom the evil spirit had been transferred, looked truly hideous, and gabbled away loudly, but did not reveal the spirit's identity.[17]

My happiness knew no bounds when the Emperor ate a little of the rice gruel I offered him.

'Is the Regent here?' he enquired. The Regent went behind the curtain of state, and explained his reasons for being present.[18]

'Has the Retired Emperor completed his move?' the Emperor asked.

'Yes, he has.'

'Go and tell him this. Nothing will be of any avail now. All I want is that the *sonshō* ritual of burning be performed at nine altars, and the confession of sins be made. Also, all the necessary arrangements must be completed by tonight. I don't feel as if I will last until tomorrow or the next day.'[19]

'But to perform such a ritual of burning is taking things to an extreme,' said the Regent.[20]

'What do you mean? Things have reached just such an extreme,' retorted the Emperor.

So the Regent withdrew, his face buried in the sleeve of his robe.[21] How sorrowful too, no doubt, the Emperor's nurses who overheard this conversation.

The Regent came back and reported, 'The Retired Emperor says that he understands, but that when you were ill last year and the year before, you expressed the same wish, and that, in view of the youth of the Crown Prince, up to now matters have been left as they are.'[22]

'Nevertheless, everything must be settled tonight,' replied the Emperor.

It was then that I realised that it was his abdication to which the Emperor had been referring.

5     Nobody slept a wink, but kept watch over the Emperor. He seemed to be in great pain, and rested his foot on me.

'Could anything ever equal this total lack of concern over the probable death, tomorrow or the next day, of somebody of my position? What do you think?' he asked.

I was so choked with tears at hearing this, that I could not reply. Perhaps my face showed signs of the strain of my vigil beside him, for he did not persist in his questioning.

He shifted his gaze to where Daini no sammi was in attendance at the threshold of the room, and said, 'You're slacking, aren't you?

Don't you realise that I'm probably going to die today or tomorrow?'[23]

'How could I ever be slacking? While I am not slacking, I only wish there were something I could do to be useful,' she replied.

'Not so. You are slacking now. I shall be keeping an eye on you to see if it happens again,' he said.

He seemed to be in such pain, that I did not leave his side for an instant, but just lay beside him, as if I were one of his nurses, and wept.

What a waste! It would be really awful if he were to die like this! I reflected on his gentle and considerate nature, which had made serving him an unmerited pleasure. Such thoughts kept sleep at bay, and so I kept watch over the Emperor.

It was the time of year when it is unbearably hot, and I was nestled in between the sliding paper door and the recumbent form of the Emperor. As I watched over his sleeping features, I could do nothing but weep. How, indeed, had I come to attend him so intimately? I thought vexedly. You can imagine my feelings as I turned over in my mind events that had taken place from the night I arrived at court up till today. I was at a loss to see the meaning of it all.

6     The sunken appearance of the Emperor's eyes on waking bore witness to the daily ebbing of his strength.

I shall keep watch over him like this, I thought, even though he seems to be asleep, for he might be frightened if he were to awake suddenly and think that everyone was asleep. This way he will see me in just the same position as before.

While I was watching over him, his eyes weakly sought mine, and he asked, 'Why are you not asleep?' I was overcome with sorrow at the very realisation that he must be able to read my inmost thoughts.

'I had a message from Sammi saying "During the Emperor's previous illnesses, he liked to be cared for by those people who normally attended him, so please take good care of him. It is too frustrating for words to be unable to attend him because of this inopportune indisposition . . .".' I replied, but was unable to continue.²⁴

'The pain is quite unbearable. I shall try doing this. It might give me some relief,' the Emperor said, placing on his chest the box from beside his pillow, in which the Sacred Jewel was kept.²⁵ The sight of his chest labouring for breath was very frightening, and I could not imagine how he could endure the pain. His breathing too came spasmodically.

Although I knew my face must look a sight, I felt I must seize this opportunity while the Emperor was awake to try offering him a little nourishment. So, shielding my face with my hand, I tried feeding him some rice gruel and *hiru*, which had been set beside his pillow. He ate a little, then fell asleep again.²⁶

7　As it drew towards dawn, I heard the sound of the temple bells. Dawn must be about to break, I thought joyfully, and then at last I heard the cawing of the crows. The sounds made by the early morning cleaners confirmed me in my impression that dawn had finally broken, and I was glad.²⁷

The other attendants will soon be awake now, I thought. They will be able to relieve me, and I shall catch up on a little sleep. In the meantime, since the shutters have been put up, and the oil-lamps lowered, I shall have a rest.²⁸

However, the Emperor saw me pulling an unlined robe over myself, and pulled it back. I understood this to mean that I was on no account to sleep, so I arose.

I withdrew to my room only when Ōidono no sammi said, 'I can look after the Emperor during the day. You go and rest.'

The person who had been waiting for me said reprovingly, 'Remember you can only tend the Emperor while you yourself are feeling fit.' However, I felt in no mood for homilies just then.²⁹

Although the Emperor's condition had been deteriorating these last few days, you can imagine my grief now that I realised that this time the end must be near. How wonderful it would be if he could be nursed back to health as he had been in his illness of the year before last.³⁰

A messenger came to call me once again, 'Please attend the Emperor.' I went to his chamber, and discovered that the reason for this summons was that they wanted to try offering the Emperor some food. Daini no sammi was propping him up from behind, and said to me, 'Offer the Emperor something to eat'. There was a minute serving on a small tray. Seeing the Emperor in an upright position, I realised that today he was really suffering and that the end was near.

The Regent was in the habit of entering the Emperor's chamber from the back, and in the normal course of events I would be well aware of his approach. Now, however, because of the Emperor's illness, everyone had fallen into the habit of moving about very quietly, so how was I to know that he was coming? How could I fail to be deeply touched by the Emperor's graciousness in warning me, in the midst of his sufferings, 'The Regent has arrived.' His kindness and presence of mind in giving me this warning, when he himself was suffering so, touched me to the heart, and tears came welling to my eyes. The Emperor gave me a dubious look, and lay down without having made any impression on his meal. Once again, I lay down beside him.

8    As the Emperor's condition was so serious, the Regent visited him without fail night and day. I felt that it was ill-mannered to be lying so openly beside the Emperor during these visits, but Lady Sammi said, 'It's the fault of circumstance. Why should you worry when the Emperor is as sick as this?' As there was nothing else for it, I remained as I was.

When the Regent came close, the Emperor drew up his knees, hiding me behind them.[31] Lying there beneath an unlined robe, I heard the Regent say, 'Some of the diviners say this, and some that. Such-and-such prayers for your recovery have been commenced. Also, the commencement of the rituals before the statue of Buddha has been postponed to the nineteenth day, as it is a propitious day.'[32]

'If I live that long,' retorted the Emperor.

At this I could hardly restrain my grief.

**9** When the Regent had withdrawn, I threw back the unlined robe which had been covering me, and was tending the Emperor, when an envoy arrived with a message from the Empress.

It read, 'When people like Sammi were attending the Emperor, I used to receive detailed reports on his condition. I am not happy about the superficial replies I am receiving now. Because of the distant connection we have, I think of you as a relative like Sammi. Please send me a detailed report on the Emperor's present condition.'[33]

'From whom is the letter,' enquired the Emperor.

'It is from the Empress,' I replied.

'Tell her to come here about noon,' he said. So I sent back such a reply.

As the Empress was to pay a visit, towards noon everyone tidied up the room, and withdrew, saying they would take a rest. However, I stationed myself close to the paper sliding-door, on the off-chance that the Emperor might require something. One never knew what sort of matters the Empress might discuss with him.

After a little while, the Emperor summoned me by tapping with his fan. The reason was to say, 'Fetch that.' When I had brought what was required, he said, 'Keep the paper sliding-door shut still.' I thought it was just as well I had stayed on, instead of retiring to my room. It appeared that there was still something he wished to discuss with the Empress, so I withdrew. As I closed the paper sliding-door, the Empress said to the Emperor, 'Just tap your fan if you want anything.' However, the sliding-door remained shut for a long time.

When the Empress returned to her palace towards evening, everyone converged on the Emperor. He looked different, perhaps because I was seeing him suddenly after a short break. My happiness was quite unparalleled at hearing him say, 'Why, today I even feel that I might live to see the dawn.'

**10** The Emperor watched quantities of ice being ladled into a metal bowl near him, and declared, 'The sight of that ice makes my spirit feel refreshed. Put all the large lumps of ice you can find into a kettle, gather everyone together, and I shall watch them being made to eat the ice.'[34]

At this all the ladies-in-waiting withdrew. Only the Regent remained in attendance. Daini no sammi, Ōidono no sammi and I went into the bed-chamber, and placed a curtain of state across the entrance.[35] Peeping out between the curtains, I saw the Regent in attendance near the threshold, while the Minister of the Centre was calling people up, and arranging them in a line near the outer bamboo blinds.[36] Among those present were the Captain of the Outer Palace Guards of the Left; the Minamoto Middle Counsellor; the Minister of the Centre's son, the Provisional Middle Counsellor; the Imperial Adviser and Middle Captain of the Inner Palace Guards; and the Major Controller of the Left.[37] They were each given a piece of ice, and then the Minister of the Centre himself took a piece, as if wishing to lend his support to this whim of the Emperor.

We, who were hiding behind the curtain of state, thought how overjoyed we would be if this enthusiasm was an indication that the Emperor was going to recover as he had in the past.

I I    As dusk had now fallen, the tall oil-lamps were lit, and as the Emperor seemed to be in great pain, the Regent and others came hurrying to his chamber.[38] There was a flurry of activity as Archbishop Zōyo and the rest were summoned.

When the Archbishop arrived, a curtain of state was positioned beside the Emperor, and I and my companions, who had slipped outside, heard him commence his incantations.[39] Perhaps as a result of this and of the chanting of the sutras, the Emperor became quiet and appeared to be asleep.

These events, as I recall, took place on the fifteenth day.

The Buddhist services continued all that night, but at dawn the Emperor seemed weaker than ever.

And so yet another day drew to a close.

I2    At dawn on the seventeenth day, Daini no sammi withdrew saying, 'I shall be off for a while. I'm going to try taking a potion for this awful pain in my chest. I shall be straight back.'

She reappeared just as dusk was falling, and after one look at the Emperor exclaimed, 'Good heavens! While I have been away, the Emperor has become all swollen.'[40]

The Emperor heard us talking and asked, 'What are you saying?'

'I was saying that during the day Your Majesty has become swollen,' replied Daini no sammi.

'Now I cannot even hear properly,' he declared, looking weaker than ever.

After a while he added, 'This time I feel there will be no deliverance for me.'

Although I felt it forward of me, I inquired, 'And what makes Your Majesty think that?'

There are no words to describe my reaction at hearing him reply, 'Because even though the Archbishop has been praying so fervently that smoke is pouring from his ears, I feel no relief as a result of his efforts, and feel, on the contrary, that my suffering is increasing.'[41]

13   At daybreak, the Minister of the Centre appeared, bearing a message from Retired Emperor Shirakawa.[42] As it was apparent that matters of some moment were to be discussed, I pretended to be asleep, since to do otherwise would have been impertinent. The Minister of the Centre explained something in detail to the Emperor. I guessed that it was to do with his abdication. When he had finished what he had to say, he came over to where I was lying, and said, 'Go back to the Emperor's side now.' He then departed.

Since yesterday, mountain ascetics from the Enryakuji had been summoned to the Palace.[43] Twelve had arrived, and they made an impressive sight as they loudly chanted their incantations.

Then, as if acknowledging that all else had failed, the Emperor summoned the Minister of the Centre, and said, 'Tell the Retired Emperor this. "Please summon that priest Gyōson whom you suggested we should try when I was ill before."'[44]

Gyōson arrived without delay, and was immediately summoned to the Emperor's bedside, where he began his supplications.

As it was the practice of priests from Miidera to revere the

*Senjukyō*, he was reading it with great devotion. I derived comfort from hearing him slowly chanting, 'May his illness be cured and may his life be long.'[45]

And so, perhaps because of the presence of so many exalted persons, all striving to outdo one another in their prayers, the evil spirit revealed itself. In a piercing voice it identified itself as Archbishop Ryū and Raigō, among others.[46]

'After your earlier visit to the temple, I thought hopefully that I might see you again. Since you did not favour me thus, I have come to bring the matter to your attention,' the spirit said.[47]

On hearing this, the Emperor replied, 'If I had enjoyed any degree of good health these last two or three years, I would certainly have paid a visit, but I have been unable even to visit places which are close at hand. If I were to recover from this illness, I should certainly pay a visit within the year.'

His sufferings seemed to intensify from that moment.

14  A messenger arrived from the Empress to say, 'I have been told that there is no sympathetic soul to bring me news of the Emperor, and I only say this to you now, because, try as I will, I can think of nobody else. Would you be able to come here straight away. I realise that there will be many people about, and that it would not be pleasant for you.'

How could I refuse to go?

'Very well,' I replied.

'Well then, come immediately,' came the reply. So I went to the Empress.

Since we were related, I was met by the envoy, and through her the Empress inquired after the Emperor's state of health.

I could not describe the Emperor as I had seen him, for I feared that there might be unfortunate repercussions if an exaggerated version of what I had said were noised abroad. Nevertheless, since I had been specially summoned in order to be asked just this, it would be remiss also not to make some sort of answer, so I said, 'The Empress must come immediately and see for herself. The Emperor looks to me to be in great pain.'

'Very well, the Empress will come if there is an opportune moment with not too many people about,' came the reply, and I was speedily sent on my way.

When I reached the Emperor's chamber, I found that a message had come from Retired Emperor Shirakawa saying 'His Majesty had best receive the Buddhist Precepts.' The Regent and Minister of the Centre had given instructions that the Master of the Buddhist Law be summoned, and were engaged in other such preparations for the ceremony.[48]

As it would certainly be daybreak by the time the ceremony was over, I said to the Emperor, 'I was summoned by the Empress, and when I went there, she said this . . .'[49]

'Getting here would not be easy,' he replied weakly, and seemed in distress.

Since the Regent himself had added, 'I think it would be nice for her to come and see you,' I decided I would urge the Empress to come immediately, before things became too hectic.

Just then Lady Sammi appeared, to say 'The Empress arrived, but she must have been told that the Regent's instructions were "The Emperor must not be left unattended," for she went away again. However, she has sent to say, "Very well, let only the Assistant Attendant remain with him."'[50]

The Regent and others all withdrew behind the paper sliding-door.

A four-foot high curtain of state was positioned near the threshold. I drew a tall oil-lamp close to the Emperor's pillow, flooding the area with light. Then I lay down beside the Emperor in the lamp-light. Although I was embarrassed at this breach of etiquette, for me to withdraw was out of the question.

'The Empress has arrived,' I announced.

'Where? Whereabout?' he asked vaguely.

My heart sank as I realised he must have lost his sense of hearing.

'Near the curtain of state,' I answered.

'Where?' he asked, pulling up the hem of the curtain.

'Here,' said the Empress.

As I guessed there were things she wanted to say to the Emperor,

I slipped away to the back of the room. When I returned, the Empress had crossed the threshold and was engaged in a long discussion about something.

Then the Regent's voice was heard saying, 'A long time has passed. It must surely be time to serve the Emperor's rice gruel.'

On hearing this, the Empress said, 'Well, in that case I shall leave now, but I'll come again tomorrow night.' So she departed.

15   I went to the Emperor's side, and offered him the usual ice and such. Then the Regent entered with some others, and said, 'Call the Master of the Buddhist Law to come in now.' He fetched the gong and other equipment from the chapel, and made preparations for the confirmation ceremony.[51]

When the Master arrived, he was separated from the Emperor only by a curtain of state.

'Fetch my robe,' ordered the Emperor, so I went and got it.[52]

I should have brought toilet articles, but since the Emperor looked as if he would be unable to raise himself up, I dampened a paper tissue and wiped his hands with it—an act which filled me with sadness. When I brought his ceremonial cap, I had such difficulty putting it on that I doubted if it would stay in place. The Emperor appeared to want to fasten the neck opening of the robe which I had put on him, but although he tried, his hands were so swollen that he was unable to do so. I was so saddened by the sight of this, that my eyes clouded over with tears and I could not see properly.

The Master rang a bell, and explained the purpose of the ceremony. 'Since this person received the Ten Precepts in a former life, and did not break one of them, he was reborn into this supreme position of Emperor, which position he has long upheld. From the past right up to the present, there has not been an Emperor to surpass him in the sincerity of his devotion to the Buddhist Law and in his compassion for all creatures. In token of tonight's ceremony, may his illness be cured and may he live to be one hundred.'[53]

Merely to hear such words convinced me that the Emperor had

made an instantaneous recovery, and I was overwhelmed with gratitude.

And so the Emperor was confirmed, replying to each Precept, 'I swear to abide by this. I swear to abide by this.' When the Regent and lords asked 'Do you say "I swear"?' the Emperor nodded his assent.[54]

16 When the confirmation ceremony was over, the Master departed, and the Emperor summoned to his bedside the son of the late Minister of the Right. He was known as the Holy Teacher Jōkai, and had long been a close attendant of the Emperor.[55]

'Let me hear you read the sutras. I have probably only tonight left to hear the voice of Jōkai,' the Emperor said. Although he seemed to be suffering terribly, he shed not a tear.

Who could fail to be moved by these words? Everyone felt that it was more than they could bear. For a time the Holy Teacher made no reply. It would seem that the reason that his voice was not heard reading the sutras was that he too was upset.

After a while I heard him softly reading the prose passage connected to the *biku* verse in the chapter, 'On Tactfulness', in the *Lotus Sutra*.[56] The Emperor listened intently, and from the point where it goes

'These dregs of the assembly, who
Because of the Buddha's splendid virtue withdrew'

he joined in, chanting smoothly and easily, without once faltering. His voice was so majestic that it quite drowned out the voice of the Holy Teacher.

It seems that the reason that the Holy Teacher specially selected that particular passage was that he had heard that the Emperor had devoted much time to memorising the first two books of the *Lotus Sutra*.

17 In the meantime, a messenger had arrived from Sammi's place.[57] She had heard of the extreme gravity of the Emperor's condition, and wanted a detailed report on the situation. Part of the message was, 'I know it is forbidden for a sick person

to attend court, but if I could just come to your room and find out about the Emperor's condition . . . .'

'This is how things are with the Emperor when you are away. Come to his chamber,' I was told, so I set forth immediately with the messenger.[58]

On reaching the Emperor's chamber, I found that Daini no sammi was supporting him from behind, while Ōidono no sammi was lying beside him just as before. I knelt down near his feet, and Ōidono no sammi said, 'I sent for you because His Majesty seems in great distress. Please hold his foot there.' So I sat holding the Emperor's foot. He wiped the perspiration from his face.

'While His Majesty is quiet like this, I shall go and attend to some business, and then return,' said Ōidono no sammi. 'Come here beside His Majesty.' So I lay down in her place beside the Emperor.

After a while the Emperor called the Holy Teacher Jōkai over close to the curtain of state as usual, and said, 'Let me hear you read the *Kannon* chapter.'[59]

The Holy Teacher read it in a most exalted manner. Then something—I know not what—prompted the Emperor to say, 'Read the verses.'[60]

When Ōidono no sammi returned, I was quite unable to move, as the Emperor's foot was resting on me and his hand was round my neck. Lady Sammi therefore settled herself near his feet, where I had been before.

I offered the Emperor some ice as usual, and he requested, 'Wipe away my perspiration.' I used some Michinokuni paper, from beside his pillow, to wipe around his sidelocks.[61] While I was doing so he said, 'The pain is quite terrible. It is because I am about to die.'[62]

'I put my faith in Amida Buddha. I put my faith in Amida Buddha,' he recited. When the Emperor was in normal health, the recitation of this phrase was avoided, even by the lowliest attendants to the ladies-in-waiting, as being inauspicious, and so hearing it clearly enunciated by the Emperor's own lips aroused a feeling of unreality, as if I were in a dream, and I could not restrain my tears.[63]

The Regent bent close to the Emperor and said, 'Pray to Buddha. Where is the copy of the *Daihannya sutra* which I have been told you made? Invoke it with all your heart.'[64]

'It must be in the chapel,' replied the Emperor.

At this the Regent went and brought a sutra to the Emperor.

'Is this it?' he asked, showing it to the Emperor.

'That is it,' he replied.

'The pain is getting worse and worse,' he cried, and was shaken by a violent spasm of coughing. 'I am going to die now. May the Ise Shrine help me.[65] I put my faith in the *Lotus Sutra* which tells of the Buddha of impartial benevolence and great wisdom.'[66] These and similar truly reverent phrases fell from his lips.

'It's agonising. I can't bear it. Hold me up,' he cried. So I arose and supported him. Up to now when we had supported him like this, he had resented our help and been difficult to manage, but now he passively accepted my assistance.

Daini no sammi was sitting behind the Emperor, and I propped his back against her, but when I took his hands, his arms were cold to the touch. I had never known such coldness at such a hot time of the year as this, and it was unnerving and distressing.

**18** The Archbishop was summoned, and also the twelve mountain ascetics. All other sounds were drowned out by their prayers.[67]

Ōidono no sammi moistened the Emperor's mouth with a hand dipped in water. He seemed oblivious of everything, intent on his earnest invocation of Amida. Every so often he would cry, 'May the Ise Shrine help me,' but this seemed to have no effect, and gradually his eyes began to take on a glazed appearance.

The Archbishop had been unable to come immediately, but appeared at last. Usually we were separated from him by a curtain of state, but now we were all clustered together without distinction, too distraught to feel embarrassed. The Archbishop, the two Ladies Sammi, the Emperor and myself—five people in all—were clustered together as if we were one.

The Archbishop, his eyes downcast, lifted up his voice in prayers of such intensity, that smoke poured from his ears. The mere sight of him alternately reproaching and entreating the Buddha was very comforting. On other occasions when the Emperor had been ill, I had managed to draw comfort from the prayers of lowly priests, so to hear someone of this eminence praying with his whole heart . . . .

'I have served Buddha for many years, for over sixty years in all, and contrary to expectations, the Buddhist Law has not yet perished. Please therefore grant the Emperor a quick recovery.'[68] He spoke as if addressing a person. 'Quickly. Quickly,' he urged, but it had no effect, and the lips which had been invoking Amida with their last failing strength, finally fell still.[69]

The Regent, recognising that all was over, said, 'It is over now. I must tell the Retired Emperor.' He called over the Minister of Popular Affairs and, raising the bamboo blind, softly told him something. When he had finished, the Minister departed.[70]

The Minister of the Centre came to the Emperor's side and said, 'There is nothing we can do now.' He straightened the Emperor's pillow and lovingly laid him down. The Regent and lords withdrew.

The Archbishop remained at the Emperor's bedside, softly and earnestly making a last address.[71]

**19** In the meantime the sun in all its splendour had intruded upon the scene. As the sun rose higher in the sky, the Emperor's face, which for days had been pallid and swollen, became clear and unblemished, and his sidelocks looked as if they had been carefully combed. In fact he looked just as if he were asleep.

The Archbishop, who had now assured himself that all was over, rose quietly to his feet, and was softly drawing open the paper sliding-door beside the Emperor, about to withdraw, when Ōidono no sammi cried, 'Alas! How sad! You are leaving, but what have you achieved? Please do something for His Majesty.'[72]

Hearing her start weeping abandonedly, everyone realised the cause and joined her. The Captain of the Outer Palace Guards of the Left; the Minamoto Middle Counsellor; the Minister of the Centre's son, the Provisional Middle Counsellor; the Emperor's foster-brothers who held the position of Middle Captain—over ten people in all—as well as all the ladies-in-waiting who had attended the Emperor, lifted up their voices and abandoned themselves to their common sorrow. So frenzied was their grief that the paper sliding-door vibrated and rocked as if there were an earthquake. A timid disposition would certainly have been unable to endure the pandemonium.

The High Court Nobles and Senior Courtiers who had been on familiar terms with the Emperor came jostling in, saying 'Let us have one last look at His Majesty.' However, those who had had little contact with the Emperor were not invited in.[73]

Daini no sammi took the hand of the seemingly sleeping figure of the Emperor, and addressed him thus, 'My Lord, how could you have gone and abandoned us all? From the moment you were born, I have never for an instant left your side. I reared you from the time you were in swaddling clothes, and accompanied you whenever you went on an imperial progress, travelling either before you or after you. When I was compelled to stay at home for just ten days because of illness, I pined for you and longed for the moment I would see you again. How then can I live hereafter without so much as a glimpse of you? Please, please take me with you. Please wake up again and let me see you. Alas! How sad! How can I carry on with this yearning in my heart? You must summon me to you.' I found this outcry hard to take.

At the sound of her voice, the mountain ascetics, who had been performing lustily, suddenly fell silent.[74] The Chief Abbot of the Enryakuji chose that moment to arrive. As he pushed open the paper sliding-door through which the Archbishop had withdrawn, Daini no sammi resumed her tearful diatribe, saying 'What good can even the Chief Abbot of the Enryakuji do now?'[75]

Someone was bundled in through the paper sliding-door, and when I looked to see who on earth it could be, I saw that the newcomer was clad in a violet-coloured jacket which I had left in my room. I realised that it was Tōzammi, who had heard the news and come to the Emperor's chamber.[76] She ranted and wept, 'Alas! How cruel! My regret is not so much that I shall never look upon

Your Majesty's countenance in the normal way with your eyes open, but that you did not summon me to come despite the ritual impurity caused by my illness. I nursed you through all your previous illnesses without fail, and I am mortified by my ill-fortune in being sick myself and unable to tend you in this your final illness.'

I just sat there beside the Emperor, pressing to my face the piece of Michinokuni paper, with which I had wiped away his perspiration. For years I had believed that my affection for the Emperor was no less than that of these people, but now I was haunted by the thought that my feelings must indeed be inferior, since I could not raise my voice in weeping as they were doing.

20   I was dimly aware of the Minister of the Centre coming in and glancing at the Emperor. The ribs of the fan he was holding rasped together as he folded and unfolded it, apparently trying to reach some decision. Then he left the room weeping.

He must have given the order for the shutters to be lowered, for straight away, despite the bright sunlight which was streaming into the room, the shutters were lowered with a clatter by the fourth rank Minor Captain of the Inner Palace Guards, Akikuni, who was the son of the Minamoto Middle Counsellor, and the Vice-governor of Kaga, Iesada, who was the son of the late Minister of the Right— apparently they were Senior Courtiers related to the Emperor.[77]

Alas! This is too much! Why have they done this? I wondered as they left. Even when the sun, heedless of my wishes to the contrary, sank in the sky as it always did, I would wait anxiously for the attendants to appear with the tall oil-lamps, mentally urging them to hurry before the shutters were lowered. And now they had lowered the shutters when the sunlight was streaming brightly into the room, and made it dark on purpose! I felt I was going out of my mind.

'This is outrageous! Why have they lowered the shutters like this? I had intended to watch over His Majesty as long as it remained light, even though there was no hope of his reviving,' cried Tōzammi, bursting into unrestrained weeping.

The Minister of the Centre reappeared, and said brokenly, 'We must change His Majesty's clothes now, and remove the padding from the mats.' He was unable to continue, but occupied himself with such tasks as fetching the Emperor's unlined robe and drawing it over him.[78]

The implicit finality of this act caused Ōidono no sammi to collapse on the lower side of the threshold, where she lay, like the Emperor, to all intents and purposes not breathing.

Seeing this, the Minister of the Centre called their son, the Middle Counsellor, and said, 'Help her away from here.' The Middle Counsellor and her own ladies-in-waiting tenderly and compassionately carried her away.

Meanwhile Daini no sammi too had been gathered up and carried away by various people, including her sons, the Governors of Harima and Izumo.[79]

21 Meanwhile Tōzammi, who was obviously weakened by her illness, had been babbling incessantly from the moment she had been bundled into the room. Although such grief-stricken behaviour was natural enough, the Minister of the Centre must have thought she was becoming too overwrought, for he looked over at her son, the Governor of Kaga, and said, 'Please assist her away from here.'[80]

'She is looking extremely weak.'

'This is all too much for me. Please stand by me,' Tōzammi said to me.

'We have no alternative. Please come to the women's quarters,' I said, trying to tug her away.[81]

'What are you saying? No words can describe my bitterness at His Majesty's dying without granting me one last glimpse of that beautiful face of his.' She was extremely overwrought, weeping and moaning and seeming to feel that someone was to blame for what had happened. Yet I could sympathise with her.

When I touched the Emperor's arm, it felt cold, but was still soft like that of a living person. I was gripped by the fleeting thought that perhaps . . . . If only he were to revive, even for a moment,

76

and say something to me. Accordingly, I could not bring myself to force Tōzammi to leave, and we sat together, holding the Emperor's arm. Imperceptibly, however, the arm stiffened.

Thinking that there was nothing to be gained by staying any longer, I said, 'Well then, let's go. There is no point in staying any longer. I only waited in the hope that His Majesty might utter another word.'

I tried to pull her away, but she clung to the Emperor, crying, 'How could I go and leave His Majesty all alone?'

Since the Governor of Kaga was disinclined to carry his mother away when she was acting like this, I said to him, 'If you do not feel up to helping your mother away, I shall call some of my ladies-in-waiting.'

At this, Tōzammi, who seemed completely out of her senses, immediately objected, 'How could you call servants to come into my lord's chamber?' She burst into hysterical weeping. As she had been assisted into the Emperor's room by just such people, I felt that this objection indicated that she had completely taken leave of her senses. Therefore I summoned some of my own ladies-in-waiting, and she was carried away on the backs of the ladies-in-waiting—dragged off as it were willy-nilly.

After the nurses had left, I and Inaba no naishi, who of all the Junior Assistants had served the Emperor with especial devotion, remained for a long time close by his side.[82]

'How fitting that, of all the people who attended His Majesty, it was you, who were so close to him, who served him to the end.' She rambled on in this fashion, and her tear-drenched face made me too feel like weeping. It was hard to stand the strain.

One of my attendants came rushing along breathlessly, and panted, 'Come quickly. Lady Sammi has fainted away.' She dragged me off to my room. Lady Sammi had indeed stopped breathing, just as if she were dead.

When dusk fell, we assembled Lady Sammi and her attendants, packed them into a carriage, and sent them home.

**22** Where the Emperor lay, all was still. When had the change taken place? For days it had been a hive of activity, with illustrious visitors and so much noise that you could hardly hear yourself speak. The hush made me aware of how appropriate to the circumstances was the expression, 'The flame has been snuffed out', and I myself observed the silence.

From Daini no sammi's room, which was separated from mine by only a single partition, came the sound of weeping. Above this lamentation, which had been going on all day, Sammi's voice could be discerned, tearfully repeating the refrain, 'Alas! When twilight deepened as it is doing now, I used to fuss about, waiting for the order for the shutters around the Emperor's chamber to be lowered immediately. What on earth am I to do, now that that order will not be given? Someone please help me! Please, my Lord, summon me to the place where you have gone. Oh! Oh!'

The sound of her lamentations increased the strain upon me.

**23** From the direction of the Daytime Chamber, came the clattering sound of things being dismantled, and the sound of many voices. While I was trying to work out what these sounds meant, my relative who shared my room when she was at court, came rushing in, incoherent with tears. The mere sight of her made me feel even closer to breaking down, without having asked what the matter was.

After a while she calmed herself, and what she had to say was, 'Alas! How thoughtless can they be! They are bustling about, saying they must transfer the Sacred Jewel and Sword to the new Emperor straight away. They are moving all the furnishings from the Daytime Chamber, and taking the Sacred Treasures and the mirrors from inside the curtain-dais. That noise is the sound of them dismantling the dais.'[83]

At this my sorrow got the better of me and I broke down and wept.

24 Mino no naishi had arrived about noon, having been charged by the Regent to take immediate care of the Sacred Sword.[84] We talked about things that had happened in the Emperor's lifetime. Since I knew nothing about the Imperial Dining Room I could not be expected to make much of her story.[85]

# BOOK TWO

25 Time passed, and the tenth month was upon us.
'There is a letter from Ben no sammi,' I was told.

When the letter was brought in to me, I read—'Retired Emperor Shirakawa must have been well apprised of your devotion to duty over the past few years at court, for he has announced, "There is a crying need for people like her to attend the Emperor. Let her come at once to court." I would therefore beg you to comply with this request.'[86]

This was so unexpected, and came as such a shock, that I thought my eyes must be deceiving me. I was aware that similar requests had been made during Emperor Horikawa's lifetime, and presumed, from the manner in which he had ignored them, that he considered them unwarranted. In view of this, it would be completely unfeeling of me to present myself at Emperor Toba's court as if I had been waiting on such a summons.

I felt the truth of the poem, said to be written by Suō no naishi, on being summoned by Emperor Go-Sanjō to attend court on the seventh day of the seventh month, when the death of Emperor Go-Reizei was still fresh in her memory—

> The flow of the Heavenly River
> Is the same, I have heard—
> Yet how sorrowful still am I,
> Faced with the crossing.[87]

I should like to see the young Emperor, I thought, as a reminder of his father, but to go to court now is just out of the question. Even when I first went to court, I had many reservations about such a gay life, but as my parents and Lady Sammi and the rest thought it a good idea, I deemed it best not to voice my feelings, but kept them to myself, and felt as deranged as the seaweed gathered by the fishermen.[88]

Even though the alternative to court life could quite truthfully be described as completely contrary to my inclinations, nevertheless, if the Retired Emperor were to hear that I had renounced the world and become a nun, he would surely not consider me so indispensable. I felt, in my confusion, that new worries were following fast on the heels of my recent trials and tribulations.

I must find some way of becoming a nun. But then, I seem to remember that even in old romances, people who capriciously have their heads shaved are criticised by the world in general as being 'superficial'. And that in fact is how I myself feel about the matter. And so I could not in all conscience opt for that way out. It would be good if I were to fall into a decline on account of all these worries. Then my illness would provide a good excuse . . . .

I worried on like this for days. There was another letter, to say, 'The Emperor's nurses are all still of the sixth rank, and it is not done for the Emperor's meals to be served by anyone under the fifth rank. The twenty-third, twenty-sixth and twenty-eighth days of this month are lucky days. So hurry! Hurry!' I read this letter over and over again, but could not reach a decision.[89]

Even during the reign of the late Emperor, I became so emaciated and unattractive as a result of the mental anguish over my private affairs, that I hesitated to venture into company. I was completely preoccupied with my own predicament. However, the Emperor was so understanding, and everyone was so good to me, on account of Sammi's having been at court for some time, that I did not want to upset anyone by leaving. Since I was for a time completely preoccupied with my own worries, trifling as they may have been, perhaps if I were to reenter court service, I would again be unable to concentrate on the job in hand, just as I had been in the past. The new Emperor is very young. Probably he would not be able to look on me tolerantly as someone who had become set in her ways. And if that were the case, and I just lived in a state of nostalgia

for the past, I would certainly be criticised by those who saw me.
I continued to be absorbed by such thoughts, and my sleeve
became quite drenched with tears.

> Ah, this dear black sleeve
> Drenched though it be with tears—
> How I cherish it
> As a keepsake of my lord.[90]

**26** So time passed. I recalled how, when I was in service, it
had been almost impossible to enjoy these quiet breaks at
home, for after about five or six days, there would be a letter from
the Palace Attendants' Office saying, 'We are short-staffed. Please
come.' While I spent my time engrossed in such thoughts, the talk
of the town was the accession ceremony.[91]

I heard that Imperial Nurse Dainagon had been allocated the
task of raising the curtains around the throne, and that she had gone
to consult Tōzammi—acting on the advice of her husband, the
former Governor of Aki, who said, 'It was Lady Sammi who was
in charge of the curtains at the accession of the late Emperor
Horikawa, so you must take a lesson from her.' Then I heard that
her father, the Major Counsellor, who had been suffering ill-health
for some time, had suddenly taken a turn for the worse and died.
What a world of sorrows we live in! I thought gloomily.[92]

In the evening I heard from Lady Sammi that the task of raising
the curtains had fallen to me. The news took me completely by
surprise, for I had imagined that my stolid silence over the last
few days had convinced Retired Emperor Shirakawa that I did not
want to return to court. Now it seemed that I was being forced
into returning, and there was nothing I could do about it.

I called the person on whom I usually relied for advice, and asked,
'I have received such and such instructions from the Retired
Emperor. What am I to do?'

'What are you to do? What a complicated world we do seem to
live in. But it looks as if you must make up your mind without
delay. It might be unfortunate for you in the long run, if you
decline to go. You must look on this, my dear, as the working
out of your destiny.'

While I was listening to this advice, a messenger arrived to tell me, 'A messenger has come from the Director of the Palace Treasury,[93] bearing the following imperial order, which originated in an order from the Retired Emperor to the Regent, "If the lady has been given mourning robes for the late Emperor Horikawa, she must discard them at once." You must change at once.'

I could not do as I wished even when it came to wearing mourning. It would be heart-breaking to discard my mourning clothes before the appointed date. I found myself comparing my lot to that of the parsley picker referred to in the old song.[94]

My elder brother, who had heard the foregoing conversation, exclaimed, 'Ah, how I, as a man, should like to receive such an imperial order. I am green with envy that the Retired Emperor should hold you in such esteem. Being a woman, you could do without such favours. I think it rather strange that, when people who had spent long years in court service during the reign of the late Emperor Horikawa, and also his foster-brothers and such-like people, were given mourning clothes to wear, you were included in that number, even though you had not been long at court,[95] and that now in the reign of this Emperor, you are again regarded as being so indispensable that an imperial order comes saying, "Discard your mourning clothes," even before the end of the mourning period.'

I was filled with disgust and shame at this outburst.

When Emperor Kazan renounced the world to become a priest, I recollected, the Lay Priest Kaneie had taken up the matter of the Controller, Koreshige, with Emperor Ichijō. Koreshige, however, even after receiving the imperial order, 'Continue as before in the position of Controller,' knew that even in these circumstances he would still be haunted by memories of his time in the service of Emperor Kazan, and consequently gave up his official post and court rank to become a Master of the Buddhist Law.[96] Should I then, with all my memories, return to court, none the wiser for my embarrassing experiences there in the past? Why, of all the ladies-in-waiting at court, should it fall to my lot to act out the unwelcome role of attendant to two generations of Emperors. I reflected ruefully that this situation must be the result of my *karma* from a previous existence. Accordingly, since there is no escaping one's destiny, I resigned myself to my fate, and purified myself with water scooped from the river. I felt refreshed in body and spirit.[97]

I tried to console myself with the thought that this extraordinary *karma* of mine must be responsible for my coming to serve the new Emperor intimately as my lord and master.

My attendants had grown accustomed over the last few years to the gay life at court, and found the prospect of seclusion at home, with no hope of returning to court, very disagreeable. They seemed very cheerful then, when they heard what had transpired, and the sight of their rejoicing made me feel cross and resentful.

And then the eleventh month was upon us.

27 I had intended making my customary pilgrimage to the Horikawa Palace on the nineteenth day, but the snow lay deep from the previous night's fall, and was still falling thickly.[98]

As there was not much time left until the accession ceremony, my entire household, it seemed, was busily engaged on the necessary preparations, working day and night, without ever stopping for a chat. So nobody had any sympathy for me when I persisted in my desire to attend the memorial service, despite the general view that we should stay home and miss it since we were so busy.

'Just go right ahead and disrupt all our preparations. The Retired Emperor and the Minister of the Centre would probably not be unduly impressed by your presence today. Even if you do not go, the skies will not fall. The snow appears to be falling so heavily, that you will not be able to find the road. It would probably not be too bad for you, riding inside the carriage, but how would your escort get on?' So my attendants grumbled on, until they ran out of objections.

'I would certainly stay home if I were only going to make a good impression on other people, but this is the monthly anniversary, and we ought not to miss it just because we are busy. Would it be right to use these preparations as an excuse for not going, even in the event that they were on account of a joyous, happy occasion?

If any of you feels the slightest pity for me, please say you will come today,' I pleaded.

My pallor as I spoke must have made them realise how important this was to me, for those I had addressed said, 'If you are so set on this idea, far be it from us to stand in your way. Bring round a carriage.'

While an escort was being assembled, it occurred to me that this was the time the ceremony usually began. As it was getting later every minute, I thought that it looked as if I would not go in the end. Then, just when I was about to give up in despair, someone said, 'Your escort is here. Hurry up.' Happily I climbed into the carriage.[99]

The snow really was falling unbearably thickly on the way. It found its way into the carriage, and the heads of the servants and ox-drivers all became white. The white backs of the oxen transformed them into white oxen. When we reached Second Avenue, the road leading to the Horikawa Palace was completely obliterated by snow.[1]

When we arrived, everyone exclaimed admiringly, 'Oh, how wonderful! When it got later than usual, we all said to each other, "It looks as if she can't make it today. And that's not to be wondered at. She must be very busy with her preparations." But you are more single-minded than most. Fancy coming today!'

And so the eleventh month was soon behind us.

28   On the first day of the twelfth month, in the darkness before dawn, I arrived at the Daigokuden. The carriage drew up at the Office of the Guards at the Western Gate, and I went across a path of straw mats into a room set aside as a waiting room.[2]

In the first grey light of dawn, the ridges of the tiled-roof palaces swam together out of the mist. I recalled the fleeting impression I had received as I passed this way on my previous arrival at the Imperial Palace.[3] My reverie was interrupted by the appearance, through the Northern Gate, of a procession of girls, clad in white ceremonial robes.[4] They were bearing a long chest, which contained dark-red women's robes.[5] I thought they presented a quite magnificent spectacle, but then my impressions were probably heightened by the whole atmosphere in which I found myself, for such a sight in itself would not have warranted any special interest.

My attendants were round-eyed with excitement, but while they were taking a lively interest in everything and obviously deriving great pleasure from the proceedings, there was I, unable to raise any enthusiasm at all.

My gaze was drawn towards the south, where it was met by the sight of the customary array of standards—the Imperial Sun Crow, others whose emblems were unfamiliar to me, and the military banners.[6] I felt I must be dreaming. When I had read about such occasions in books such as *Eiga Monogatari*, I had returned again and again to the description of such scenes, trying to visualise it for myself. So you may well imagine my feelings on finding myself a witness to a vivid enactment of such a scene.[7]

When the sun was high in the sky, a clamour arose that the Emperor had arrived.[8] The lords and nobles were there with their retainers, some wearing their ceremonial jewelled caps, others wearing brocaded sleeveless over-robes. The officers of the Inner Palace Guard were attired in what I believe is called their 'ceremonial armour.' Although I had never seen these costumes before, I was amazed to find that I knew them from the Chinese scenes decorating the paper sliding-doors in the Emperor's Daytime Chamber.[9]

Then came the moment when the Assistant Captain of the Outer Palace Guards, looking most imposing and reminiscent rather of Bishamon, told me 'It's your turn now. Hurry. Hurry.'[10] As if in a dream, I mounted the steps to the throne, and felt dazzled, in spite of myself. I went through the motions of raising the curtain with my hand. Then a court lady, her hair piled high, came forward and pinned it in place. The ritual could obviously have been performed without my participation. Why should I have been bothered with this formality? I wondered.[11]

The Emperor was decked out very prettily, but the sight of him seated upon the Imperial Throne was a severe shock to me. A haze swam before my eyes, and, I am ashamed to admit, I felt so distressed that I could not look at him directly. When the ceremony was over, I slipped away, back to the waiting-room.

As soon as night fell, I left for home. When I arrived, looking and feeling half-dead, the family, who had been waiting for me, took dubious note of my expression, and burst into questions such as 'What has happened to make you look so pale?' The realisation that my face still betrayed my inmost feelings was too much for me, and I burst into a flood of tears.

**29** The twelfth month dragged to its end.

'There is a letter from Ben no suke,' someone called. When the letter was brought to me, I read as follows, 'Retired Emperor Shirakawa has pronounced that, as Ben no sammi and Dainagon no suke are unable to be present at court this New Year's Day, and as it is desirable that the Emperor should be attended by as many qualified people as possible on such a day, you must come to court.'[12]

As there was no avoiding such a summons, I agreed to go, and set about making preparations for departure.

I arrived at the Palace towards evening on New Year's day.[13] From the moment my carriage went through the gates, I was assailed by memories of the past, and was overcome with grief. While I was settling into my room, I discovered that the Emperor had gone elsewhere, so that night passed uneventfully.

When I arose next morning, I found that there had been a heavy snowfall overnight. It was still snowing hard. When I looked over at the Emperor's quarters, I felt that nothing particular had changed. Then just when I felt that everything was conspiring to convince me that the late Emperor was still here, I heard a childish voice singing, 'Fall, fall, powder-snow!'[14]

'Who can that be? Whose child is it?' I was wondering. Then it hit me—it must be the Emperor! How absurd! If this is the master whom I am to regard as my lord and protector, I am certainly not filled with a sense of security, I thought desolately.

I felt on edge all day, and when dusk fell, I went to the Emperor's chambers. Someone arrived to tell me, 'Today is a lucky day, so you may serve the Emperor his meal for the first time.' She dimmed the tall oil-lamps in the Emperor's room, and beckoned me, 'Over here.' As I moved forward silently to receive the Emperor's meal, I felt that nothing had changed. However, the sombre black tray, set out with unglazed earthenware bowls instead of the covered lacquered bowls, was new to me.

The Emperor came running into the room, and peered into my face.

'Who is this?' he asked.

'This is the daughter of Emperor Horikawa's nurse,' was the reply, and he accepted this as the truth. I observed that he was more grown-up than when I had seen him before.[15]

I remembered the occasion vividly. It occurred the year before last, when the Crown Prince was staying at the Imperial Palace. He was residing in the Kokiden, and had gone to the Seiryōden to visit his father.[16] After some time, Emperor Horikawa had said encouragingly, 'Well now, it's time for you to go home. I must have my hair arranged before it gets dark.'

'I should like to stay with you a little while longer,' the Prince had said, and the Emperor's fond expression had reflected his pleasure in his son's sweetness. The memory plunged me into gloom.

I remained all that night beside the Emperor, and was touched by how sweet he looked as he lay there innocently, quite lost among the bed-clothes.

30 Everyone rose at daybreak, and when I looked about me, I noticed that the blinds in the Emperor's room were made of very coarse rushes, and that the border material was slate-grey in colour. The curtains of the screen of state, which served the purpose of a room-divider, were of the same slate-grey, while the frame was of whitewood. The special chair used when dressing the Emperor's hair was also missing. I presumed its absence was due either to its being unnecessary during this period of mourning, or to the Emperor's youth.[17] When I served the Emperor his meal, I was touched to see how eagerly he ate.

About noon, the Regent arrived and everyone withdrew.[18]

Should I, too, stop serving the Emperor his meal and withdraw? I wondered. When I had been attending Emperor Horikawa, who was an adult, I had not hesitated to withdraw in such circumstances. And moreover, the Emperor had been of an age to warn me of the arrival of such notables. I decided to remain where I was, since I would surely be criticised were I to abandon this little fellow half-way through his meal. All that time I spent in the service of Emperor Horikawa, I quite failed to appreciate the tremendous consideration he showed me, so the least I can do now is to cherish his memory.

I prostrated myself, very much aware of my breach of etiquette, and heard the Regent inquire of those outside, 'Who is that in there?' They must have told him that it was I.

The Regent entered the room through the sliding-door, and came forward on his knees.

'How long have you been at court? From now on I should like you to remain with the Emperor as you are doing now. And besides, I miss the late Emperor and keep remembering the good old times, and now I shall be able to console myself by talking them over with you.' He continued in this vein—it was all very sad. It seemed that we were both of the same mind.

I recalled that on one occasion in the past, the Emperor was reputed to have asked, 'Who is to serve my meals today?', and that, on being told whom it was, he had stuck out his tongue, girded up his silk trousers, and fled.[19] Apparently everyone had thought this a great joke and laughed uproariously. It was the Regent who was to serve the Emperor's meal on that occasion.

I was thus at a loss for a reply, and remained silent. The Regent continued, 'How unexpected this is! I never imagined I would be able to approach you like this, and talk things over with you. When I visited the Emperor when he was ill, and you were lying beside him, he drew up his knees and hid you behind them, didn't he? At that time I certainly never expected to see you again under these circumstances. Yes, the Emperor did indeed hide you behind his knees, and now he too is hidden from us. Well, such is life!'

With this he withdrew, but I shared his sentiments, and felt overcome with sorrow.

So passed a joyless New Year. And with its passing, people, depending on their involvement with the past, began wearing lighter-coloured robes.

**31** I saw no reason to miss the late Emperor's memorial service this month, just because it was the first month of the year. When I arrived at the Horikawa Palace, everyone exclaimed, 'How did you manage to get here? We heard you were at court. And here were we thinking that you would certainly not come this month . . . .'

'How could I stay away? I have vowed to serve the Emperor to the end. And I came here even when I was in the middle of all those preparations for the accession ceremony, didn't I?' I retorted.

'Yes, indeed. It is very noble of you to come unfailingly like this,' they agreed.

'The Empress is having flowers offered to the *Lotus Sutra*, to try and comfort her in this trying time,' they explained, as they went about their preparations. I found it all very moving.[20]

**32** The second month came and I attended my loved one's anniversary service.[21] From my position near the paper sliding-door I could hear the voice of the priest delivering the address, but as my eyes roamed about me, the thought uppermost in my mind was another occasion.

It was the first month of another year. I was in attendance at court, but someone had been sent to collect me as the *shushō* ceremony was going to be held.[22]

'It's a pleasant spot. Why don't you come along with me?' I was invited. So I set off in the company of Taifu no suke and Naishi.[23]

I became aware of someone beside this very paper sliding-door, and exclaimed, 'So here you are! I came along with Lady Taifu no suke and Lady Naishi.'

'I am delighted to have the pleasure of meeting Lady Naishi,' said that other, as we all met.

Then she continued, 'I cannot thank you enough for the marvellously unstinting way in which you have looked after Lady Sanuki here. Now that I have retired from the world, I am so ashamed of my appearance, that I will not set foot abroad. And so I have not even been to visit you. Besides which, dressing myself up to sally forth would be quite unbecoming. I have been brooding on how I was to fulfil my desire of retiring from the world this month, and I feel that this meeting is a sign from Buddha. What a happy moment this is! Now, with my mind at rest, and having been led to an understanding of the meaning of things, I can look forward to a peaceful existence in the world to come.'

At the time I had wondered why she was so concerned about the world to come.[24]

And so the second month too passed.

33    The third month came, and as usual I went to the Palace for the memorial service. The blossoms around the Horikawa Palace were very beautiful. I understood the feelings of Kanekata, at the death of Emperor Go-Sanjō, expressed in the poem

> True indeed
> That flowers have no feelings!
> For here they are blooming
> With colours bright as ever.

The colours of the blossoms did indeed appear as bright as ever.[25]

The former Seiryōden had been converted into a Buddha Hall, and until the seventh month religious services would be duly performed at set times morning and evening. Various areas such as the quarters of the twenty members of the Emperor's Private Office and the guard-room of the Inner Palace Guards of the Left, had become priests' quarters.[26] As I gazed at this sad vestige of what had been the Imperial Palace, I understood the sentiment contained in the poem, said to have been written by Jōtōmon'in on seeing the Palace, silent and still—so different from before, after the death of Emperor Ichijō.

> The Jade Tower—
> Who could have so described
> This cloud palace where lingers
> No shadow of royalty?[27]

The Empress had instructed that the Thirty Readings be conducted, and each day in her apartments, a chapter of the *Lotus Sutra* was read.[28]

I accompanied Lady Sammi to one of these readings. At its conclusion, Lady Sammi obeyed the Empress' request to present herself.

The Empress overheard the manner in which her request was delivered by her attendant, who went by the name of Saishō, 'Lady Sammi, will you please come over to the Empress. I feel uncomfortable when Lady Suke is around these days, though.'

She remonstrated, 'But Suke has demonstrated the depth of her feelings. She has come faithfully to this dreary place which must hold no attraction for her. . . .' She was unable to continue, and the sound of her choking sobs was more than I could bear. When dusk fell, we left.

At the end of the month, I attended court.

**34** When the fourth month arrived, and with it the occasion of the seasonal change into summer clothing, everyone went to watch the women servants as, heedless of their own appearance, each strove in time-honoured manner to out-shine the others in her struggles to change the drapes of the curtains of state. I, however, felt no desire to go and watch, for I remembered how Emperor Horikawa had delighted in watching the performance.[29]

When the anniversary of the Buddha's birth came round, everyone tried to outdo one another in the offerings they presented. When the ceremony commenced, the bamboo blinds were lowered in the Daytime Chamber where the Emperor was enthroned, and everyone moved forward to get a good view.[30]

The High Court Nobles, headed by the Regent, were seated in a row along the outer ante-room, the trains of their under-robes arranged over the balustrade in time-honoured fashion.[31]

The officiating priest explained the meaning of the ceremony, and sprinkled water on the Buddha-image. The mountain-shaped cones and the five coloured waters were the same as always.[32] After the priest had sprinkled water, the Regent advanced and sprinkled water. He was followed in turn by the High Court Nobles, who all sprinkled water.

Everything was just as it had always been. But when the Captain of the Outer Palace Guards of the Left and the Minamoto Middle Counsellor stepped forward to sprinkle water, they seemed quite overwhelmed by their burden of grief.[33] Their very faces seemed altered. It was all so depressing, that I too could not restrain my sorrow. However, as I had no intention of making a public display of myself, I pulled the imperial curtain of state closer to me and watched from behind its shelter. However, the young Emperor decided he wanted to see over the top of the curtains, and as he was not tall enough, I had to lift him up in order for him to see. He was very sweet. Emperor Horikawa, being an adult, would have been in front of the curtain-dais, attired in his ceremonial robes, making invocations to the Buddhas and scriptures.

Realising that I would be conspicuous with my tear-stained face, which must be no less melancholy than that of the Middle Counsellor, and not wanting to make a spectacle of myself, I withdrew from the Emperor's presence before the ceremony was over.

35 At dusk on the fourth day of the fifth month, I was watching the eaves of the Palace buildings being decked with irises in preparation for the Iris Festival, when I recalled how on this day last year—I had no sad memories then—the palanquins loaded with irises had been carried into the courtyard in front of the Breakfast Room. Then servants had swarmed over the roof of each building, thatching them so thickly with irises that it seemed they must have denuded even the famous Mizu Fields of irises.[34]

The very next day the sky was full of rain-clouds, and as I watched the constant dripping of water from the irises decorating the eaves, my sole thought was

> The irises decorating the eaves
> Wet with early summer rain,
> And my sleeves wet with tears—
> Reflections of this gloomy sky!

The days passed, until we were at the middle of the month.

I recalled how, during Emperor Horikawa's reign, I had learned that preparations were in progress for the *Saishō* Lecture, and how, from the middle of the month, when the lecture was over, the Emperor would often refer to points which had arisen in the debate following the lecture, and would remark on the magnificence of the occasion during the course of our own leisurely conversations.[35]

36 The sixth month came and the heat was stifling. My main preoccupation, nevertheless, was the past.

This time last year there was no indication of the Emperor's impending sickness. He was relaxed and in good spirits. When he was consulted about the proposition that everyone visit Horikawa Springs, he sent a messenger urging everyone to go by all means.[36]

'His Majesty approves the idea, so let us go, without delay, tomorrow,' it was decided. I was sent on ahead to await the arrival of the others. They came in two ox-drawn carriages. We spent an enjoyable day at the Springs, and when it came time to return, I decided I would not return to court, but would remain in this idyllic spot.

However, a lady-in-waiting by the name of Lady Hitachi, discovered that I was staying and remonstrated, 'You just can't do this. For heaven's sake, come back to the Palace. The Emperor has announced, "I am going to get everyone playing fan-lottery." He is providing all the fans, and will be waiting for us.' So I accompanied the others back to the Palace.[37]

The Emperor was waiting for us, and asked all sorts of questions about the Springs.

'Well now, how about a game of fan-lottery tonight?' he suggested.

'I would like to play tonight, since it seems so long until the morning, but it would be a shame, wouldn't it, if we were to miss the expressions on people's faces because of the dark,' I said.

So we began the game early the next morning, as soon as dawn had broken. The Emperor called us into position. Although everyone was there, with Lady Daini no sammi at our head, the Emperor had to pick on me.

'You first. Draw a fan,' he told me. So I drew one, but I missed the beautiful one I had had my eye on, and ended up with the worst fan of the lot. I flung it down in front of the Emperor.

'Have you ever seen such behaviour?' he said, bursting into laughter.

And somebody called Lady Tajima remarked, 'It is the behaviour one would expect from a houseman. Nobody else could get away with it.'[38] Everyone joined in the merriment, and I gave no thought to the incident at the time.

Now, however, I wondered how I could ever have behaved like that, for it was most ill-mannered, and I realised how unworthy I had been of the Emperor's consideration.

37  The seventh month came round again. Everyone was bustling about preparing for the ceremonies to mark the end of the twelve months' mourning. When the day of the anniversary of Emperor Horikawa's death arrived, the ceremonies were conducted by one hundred priests, just as for the forty-ninth day ceremony last year. As the proceedings were the same, I shall not describe them.[39] After the ceremony last year, six ladies-in-waiting had stayed on at the Horikawa Palace. The Empress would be in good hands, but these ladies-in-waiting were all lamenting, 'How lonesome and sad we feel, now that the time has come for us to take our leave. While we have been in attendance here, we would await your monthly visit for the memorial service, and as soon as it was over, we would start counting the days to the next visit, wishing that the time would pass quickly. So it is hard to bear the thought that this meeting is to be our last.' Their grief knew no bounds. Lady Sammi slipped away while they were still lamenting.

The following day somebody said to me, 'The lady-in-waiting called Izumo wrote this poem and attached it to a plume of pampas grass from the northern courtyard—

> As we bid farewell
> And go our separate ways
> This autumn evening,

The very tips of the pampas grasses
Are wet with dew.'

Just to hear of this, filled me with desolation.[40]

3 8    On the twenty-fifth day, when all the memorial services
were over, everyone changed out of their mourning clothes.
The furnishings which had been used up to now in the Emperor's
chambers—the coarse-textured blinds, drapes of the screens of state,
and sliding-doors—were removed. Also, the curtain-dais which up
to now had been missing from the Imperial Bedchamber, was
re-erected just as it used to be. The furnishings were just as in the
past, with not a single alteration, and the effect was magnificent.

First the Regent, followed by the Senior Courtiers and Chamberlains, changed out of mourning, and untied the ribbons on their
ceremonial caps.[41] There was a splendid array of ladies-in-waiting,
decked out in all the colours of the rainbow, for each had tried to
outshine the others, just as if nothing had ever happened.[42] I thought
it strange that a change of date could bring about such a complete
change. Everyone was involved, right down to those ladies who
were fussing, 'We must change the white hairpins and hair-cords
we have been using for the normal mottled ones.'[43]

The Regent arrived at the Palace, magnificently attired. He
summoned me to go to the Emperor's room at once. When I
presented myself, the two of us changed the Emperor's clothes. We
dressed him very smartly in an everyday robe with train. But even
while I was fixing the train, the thought uppermost in my mind
was how, in the past, I used to arrange the Emperor's clothes
before he set forth each morning to offer his prayers before the
limestone altar.[44]

'The official supervising the change from mourning clothes has
arrived at the Palace. It is time you were changed,' the Regent said
to the Emperor. 'Hurry! Hurry!' he urged.

As I could not be the only one at court still wearing mourning,
I went and changed.

When I reached my room, however, I felt not the slightest
inclination to change. I regarded these mourning clothes as a keep-

sake of the late Emperor, and to abandon them would mean losing that keepsake. I felt very forlorn.

Everyone—those who had loved the Emperor, and those who had no particular feeling—had worn mourning clothes, and they had all changed out of them at the same time, even those who had been in close attendance upon the Emperor. I knew that one could not do as one liked in a matter such as this, but it still did not make the thought of changing any less disagreeable. However, I could not wear mourning for ever, so I resigned myself and changed.

When Emperor Nimmyō died, Bishop Henjō became a priest and went into seclusion, but the following year, when everyone changed out of their mourning clothes, he is said to have written

> Now, when one and all
> In flower-hued robes are decked,
> Would that the tears that wet
> These sombre sleeves might dry![45]

39 And so the eighth month came, and the twenty-first day was fixed for the move to the Imperial Palace. Everyone plunged busily into the preparations for the move.

Naturally, I did not want to go, for I feared that when I saw the interior of the Imperial Palace, just the same as it used to be, I might not be able to hold back the tears which would be so out of place on the Emperor's first visit. However, I received a message from Lady Sammi, 'Retired Emperor Shirakawa has ordered that all suitable people are to be present. Please come.'

'If there has been such an order, I shall just send the girl attendants to carry the fire and water at the head of the procession, but I don't think I shall go myself,' I remarked.[46]

'I agree there is a point in what you are saying, but it would look bad if you were not to go, having once been summoned. You will just have to put up with it, for you really must go,' I was advised.

As I was being forced into going, I set out, but I was very much aware that this was the last thing I wanted to do.

On the day of the move, the Minister of the Centre arrived at the Palace to dress the Emperor's hair in the *mizura* style. The bamboo blinds in the Breakfast Room were rolled up, and I was amazed to see how composed the Emperor looked as the Minister bound up his hair.[47]

When it was quite dark, the procession set out.[48] I was one of the Emperor's escort, and in due course we arrived at the Palace. From the moment we passed through the Central Gate, I felt overcome with melancholy, just as I had expected.[49]

Once, when I had been passing by this gate on the way to the Kōryūji,[50] and had a fleeting glimpse of the Palace buildings beyond it, I had thought to myself, 'This is the gate I used to pass through morning and evening. Then, soon after the twentieth day of the twelfth month the year before last, Emperor Horikawa moved to the Horikawa Palace.[51] I accompanied him out through this gate on that occasion. I passed through it never thinking that it was for the last time. Now, come what may, I shall probably never pass through it again in this lifetime.'

And here I was, the same old self, returning to the Palace through this gate! I felt saddened and embittered.

When we reached the Palace, I found that the room allotted to me was Lady Daini no sammi's old room.

Lady Sammi appeared at noon, and said that the equipment must be taken to the Emperor's chambers. On my way there, I had to walk past the storehouse, and then ascend some steps.[52]

40    That night I again spent at the Emperor's side. As I gazed round the bedchamber, everything looked just as it had before, . . .[53] As this was the Emperor's first stay at the Imperial Palace, the water and fire brought by the girl attendants were set on either side of the Emperor's pillow. That was something which was different.

Even while I was lying beside the Emperor, I kept remembering how I had lain beside the late Emperor just like this, on nights when I was in attendance and the Empress was not visiting. I was overwhelmed with sadness. While everyone else seemed to be sleeping peacefully, I just lay there, quite unable to sleep for the myriad disturbing thoughts which kept floating through my mind.

I could hear the voices of the Imperial Guards of the Emperor's Private Office on the night-watch, as they challenged one another in the narrow alleyway beside the Imperial Bathing Room and at the doorway to the Senior Courtiers' Chamber.[54] I had never been conscious of their voices in the past, but now my ears were attuned to them. Then a sentry from the Inner Palace Guards of the Left called the hour; a voice said, 'We must look into this. It seems a bit odd;' and then came the sound of the time-board being fixed to its post. Nothing had changed—not even the marten-like movements of the Inner Palace Guards of the Left on the night-watch.[55]

Even the sight of the drapes of the curtain-dais brought back memories of Emperor Horikawa's day. Since I do nought but lament the past, I reflected, when will my dew-drenched sleeve ere be dry?[56] Indeed, this sleeve, bereft of the loved one it once entwined, is becoming ever more drenched, and one could well go fishing in the pool of tears beneath my pillow.[57]

It seemed to me that everything I looked at was exactly the same as before. All that was missing was the figure of Emperor Horikawa. How sad a realisation! As I gazed upon the sleeping form of the young Emperor, I was struck by how innocent and peaceful he looked, and how different his attitude was.

The year before last I had been in constant attendance upon the Emperor, just as I now was. Although the Emperor had recovered from a recent bout of ill-health, Retired Emperor Shirakawa sent this message, 'I beg you to take good care of yourself. Don't leave your bedchamber for a little while yet.' So, to while away the time, we would chat in an aimless way about this and that, about events past and present. On one occasion the Regent approached from behind. I rose, and was about to withdraw, as I felt that it would be ill-mannered and unseemly to remain lying where I was, when the Emperor, realising that I must be feeling that I should not be seen, said 'Stay where you are. I shall make a screen.' He bent up his knees, and hid me behind them. I recalled this considerate action as clearly as if it had only just happened.

There had come a time when the world had undergone a change, and the fact that I alone remained, as a relic from the past, among all these people who had not known that other world, must surely be the workings of some *karma* from a previous life. I mused on these thoughts, and felt completely overwhelmed with grief.

41 I rose thankfully when dawn broke. The others were all saying excitedly, 'Let's have a look at the parts of the Palace we haven't yet seen.' I knew that if I were to accompany them, countless memories of the past would be stirred up, and therefore I was just sitting vacantly doing nothing, when the young Emperor came and pulled me willy-nilly to my feet, urging 'Come on. Come on. I don't know the way to the Black Door, so you must show me.'[58]

On the way there, I saw that the Seiryōden and Jijūden were just as they had always been. And when I saw the Table Room and the screen with the scene of Lake Kommei, I felt I was meeting old friends again.[59] The Kokiden, which had previously been the residence of the Empress, now served as the Regent's quarters, when he was on night-duty at the Palace. The trees and grasses which Emperor Horikawa had planted in front of the small half-shutters of the Black Door Gallery were flourishing—growing wildly with nobody to tend them.[60] The sight reminded me of a poem attributed to Miharu no Arisuke—

> How sad to find the pampas grasses
> Planted in clumps by my loved one's hands,
> Have grown into a wilderness,
> Loud with the chirping of insects![61]

Among all the glorious rainbow-hued flowers blooming along the banks of the little stream which ran through the garden, I was especially attracted to the dark-hued bush-clover, which was just a mass of blossom, that would glitter bejewelled with the morning-dew, and flutter gently in the evening breeze.[62] But even as I enjoyed the sight, I thought how much it would have appealed to Emperor Horikawa, had he been there to see it, and I murmured to myself—

> How drenched my sleeve with tears of longing,
> When, from the Bush-clover Door I see
> The flowers we knew blooming changelessly.

I considered reciting this poem to someone, but, apart from the fact that there was nobody who shared my feelings, it would be unfortunate if others were to hear of such a poem being composed on the occasion of the Emperor's first stay at the Imperial Palace. However, the sight of the Sogyōden brought a certain person to mind. I guessed that she would be at her home, with her memories as her constant companions, so I sent her my poem.

Her reply was—

> I beg your understanding of this heart
> So wrought with memories of the past,
> That it cannot with equanimity recall
> The flowers we once enjoyed together,
> From the Bush-clover Door. [63]

'If even you, who are serving at court just as you used to, feel the way you have described, how readily imaginable then will be my feelings, as I pass the time here at home, with nothing to distract me from my memories.'

It was in such ways that I became ever more conscious of the past.

42 And so the ninth month came. On the ninth day I served at the banquet to celebrate the Chrysanthemum Festival, and then the month was half over. [64]

Gazing over in the direction of the storehouse one languid noontime, I recalled how Emperor Horikawa once decided to instruct me in the scriptures.

'I shall make a perfect copy of the sutra I have studied, and give it to you,' he said. He was engaged in his daily religious observances in the chapel, but he rose to his feet, and went and started writing. I had already gone to my room, and he must have thought that it would be thought a great joke if he were to go there with the sutra he had transcribed.

While I was reflecting on how unworthy I had been of the consideration that had been accorded me, the young Emperor appeared and demanded, 'Lift me up and show me the pictures on the sliding-doors.' Feeling my train of thought was completely shattered, I set off to show him the pictures on the sliding-doors in the Imperial Dining Room, but on the way I noticed, hanging from the walls of the Imperial Bedchamber, the tattered remains of the musical scores Emperor Horikawa had copied out and pasted there, in the hope that by constantly seeing them, he would become familiar with them. I was quite shattered by the sight.[65]

> The past is a dream
> That lingers on
> In the flautist's scores
> Clinging to the walls.

I buried my face in my sleeve to hide my grief. The young Emperor was watching me curiously, and as I did not want him to know what was upsetting me, I put on a show of unconcern, and said, 'I yawned, and it made my eyes water.'

'I know all about it,' he said.

I was taken aback by the blend of sweetness and authority in his words, and queried, 'And what is it that you know?'

'That you are probably thinking about something involving the syllables *ho* and *ri*,' he replied.

I was charmed to realise that this little boy understood all about my feelings for the late Emperor Horikawa. I felt my spirits soar, and found myself smiling.

And so the ninth month too was soon at an end.

43　　The twenty-first day of the tenth month had been set for the Great Purification for the Great Festival of Thanksgiving, and everyone was involved in preparations for the event.[66]

When the day came, the Governor of Harima, Nagazane, arrived at the Palace to arrange the Emperor's hair in the *mizura* style.[67] The Minister of the Centre rolled up the bamboo blinds in the Imperial Dining Room, and revealed the Regent, who was waiting at the threshold. Out on the verandah, the Assistant Captain of the Outer Palace Guards of the Left, resplendent in a scarlet over-robe, was directing proceedings.[68]

The dressing of the Emperor's hair was soon completed, and a Chamberlain came to report, 'The Acting Imperial Lady has arrived.'[69]

'The Emperor has heard. Let the procession begin,' the Regent said, making sure that everything was right.

When the scene was set, the Empress Mother and party appeared, all magnificently attired.[70]

**44** And so the various festivals came and went. Now it was the *Gosechi* celebrations and the Special Festival, for which everyone was preparing. As this year's *Gosechi* fell in the year of a Great Festival of Thanksgiving, everyone was saying, 'It will be quite different from usual. There will be more dancers from High Court Noble families. It should be a memorable year.'[71]

The ladies-in-waiting were all trying to sound more knowledgeable than each other—'What is known as the Attendants' Dance is a sight not to be missed. On the night of the Day of the Tiger, the Senior Courtiers are sure to be roaming all over the Palace, their ceremonial over-robes awry, as has become the custom'.[72]

They tried to get some information out of me, but I did not feel like answering.

**45** I was in the chamber used by the Empress on her visits to the Emperor, so absorbed in memories of the past as to be heedless of the current festivities.[73]

At the *Gosechi* the year before last, Emperor Horikawa had taken a much greater interest than usual in the proceedings—perhaps because he knew the festival was to be his last. He had wandered excitedly about the Palace from the moment the dancers arrived. That first night he stayed up late watching the Dais Rehearsal, and slept later than usual the next morning. However, the news that there had been a snowfall roused him, and as the Empress was with him at the time, they decided to send letters to the dancers. I was attending the Emperor that day, and helped them tie and loop the decorative hair-braids.[74]

Workmen arrived to build the customary bridge used by the dancers for the Attendants' Dance. It ran from the steps of the Shōkyōden to the steps at the north-east corner of the Seiryōden.[75] Emperor Toba was fascinated by the sight of the builders, and I stayed there with him till it grew dark. My thoughts, however, were all of the past.

Early one snowy morning, Emperor Horikawa had been roused from his slumbers by my exclaiming at what a heavy snowfall there had been overnight. I had spent the night with the Emperor, and we went together to look at the snow.

I have always been delighted by snow, but that morning it was especially wonderful. Since even the humble homes of the common people were transformed into things of beauty, how much more the Imperial Palace, which sparkled like a highly polished jewel or mirror. Had I been an artist, I would have liked to paint the scene exactly as we saw it together, so that everyone could see it.

When the Emperor pushed up the shutters, we found that the snow had indeed piled up so deeply that even when we thought we could distinguish treetops, it was virtually impossible 'to name one as a plum tree.'[76] The bamboo in the thicket in front of the Jijūden was bowed down so heavily with snow that it seemed it must have broken. Even the fire-hut in front of the Palace was buried beneath the snow, and the sight of snow still falling from that leaden sky was quite awe inspiring. I was especially impressed by the depth of the snow-drifts alongside the bamboo fence in front of the guard-house of the Imperial Guards.[77]

Perhaps because of the magic of the moment, perhaps because I was overcharged with emotion—the Emperor seemed to throw out a radiance as he stood there looking out, and I felt completely ashamed of my own sleep-ruffled appearance.

'I should look especially beautiful on a morning such as this!' I exclaimed.

The Emperor seemed amused by this, and replied, 'You should always look so.'

The memory was so strong that I felt he was there before me, smiling that same tender smile.

At the time I had been wearing—in keeping with the *Gosechi* celebrations—a set of autumn-coloured robes in shades ranging from yellow to crimson, topped by a light purple Chinese jacket.[78] The colours stood out in vivid contrast with the pure white of the snow. The total effect was splendid, and the Emperor let his gaze linger on, unwilling to hurry back inside. But just then we became aware of some people—probably servants from the guardhouse of the Imperial Guards—approaching the bamboo fence. They surveyed the snow-drifts, and we heard women's voices exclaim 'Good heavens! How terribly deep the snow is! What shall we do? We wouldn't be able to get through it even if we tucked up the hems of our skirts!'

'Listen to them! They are trying to find a solution to this terrible catastrophe that has befallen them! I feel that the wonder of the snow has been shattered,' the Emperor exclaimed, laughing.

The young Emperor, completely unaware of the fantasy world in which I was dwelling, dragged me off, chattering 'Ask for the tool that workman is using. Go on! Go on! Ask him before he leaves. Say it! Go on, say it!'[79]

His innocent enthusiasm brought me back to my senses. Keeping up with him and answering his questions took my mind off my sorrows, but when I said 'I think I shall leave now,' everyone murmured to one another, 'Well, how fantastic! Why, without even staying to see the performance?'

46 The Empress Mother was involving herself more than usual in the festivities. Chrysanthemums were fastened to the curtains—which were worked in a tri-coloured design—of the screens of state in the Narrow Corridor. From beneath these screens spilled the sleeve-openings of the robes of the ladies-in-waiting—a riot of autumnal tonings.[80]

My attention was caught by the spectacle, and I was reminded of how Emperor Horikawa, who did not as a rule become enthused about such things, had come, the year before last, to judge which was the most beautiful of the robes worn by the ladies-in-waiting assembled in the Empress' chamber.[81]

'Let everyone display their sleeves, regardless of rank. Try not to make them look as if they have been draped there on purpose, but rather as if they had just spilled down accidentally while you were sitting there,' the Emperor said, taking upon himself the task of placing the ladies in position.

'You drape your sleeve from the first bay,' he told me.

The sleeve-openings of the others were in a dark-red and green combination, whereas my Chinese jacket was in a totally different shade of purple-red, and I was worried that it would not blend with the others.[82]

'But mine doesn't look right,' I objected.

'It won't be noticed from a distance. Don't worry about it. Nobody is going to make a note of your name. They would have no idea who you were.' The Emperor had his mind set on creating a certain effect, and so tried to assure me that I was not at fault.

When everyone was in position along the edge of the Black Door Gallery, the Emperor viewed us through the small half-shutters of the Empress' Chamber.

'Let that sleeve hang out a little further. Pull that one there in a bit,' he directed. How could I help but recall the enthusiasm he radiated as he took over the arrangements that day.

I was just thinking that I would probably have to spend that night too at the Palace, when I received a message from the Regent, saying, 'Retired Emperor Shirakawa has instructed "It is customary to have two Assistant Attendants present at the *kagura* performance in the Seishodō." Ben no suke will be one. Will you agree to be the other?'[83]

It occurred to me that I could use the preparations for this performance as an excuse for leaving the Palace, so I sent word home, 'Please send somebody to collect me.' My escort arrived as dusk was falling.

47 I relaxed on the way home—even though we had set out before night had fallen—and abandoned myself to my memories of the past. Others will be baffled by all this, but if they only knew the gentle disposition of this Emperor I had served so closely!

When I was in attendance at court, I always liked to leave for home at nightfall, and could not keep my mind on my job when dusk deepened. And so I used to feel most vexed if the Emperor, knowing that I was looking forward to going, decided to delay me. He would dally about his affairs, and I recall one night in particular. He had gone to visit the Empress, and did not return until very late. I waited until his eventual reappearance, but he somehow guessed my intentions, from the way in which I urged him to finish his nightly duties, and asked if I was intending to leave for home.

'That is so,' I replied.

At this he flung himself down, exclaiming 'I shall leave all the work I have to do tonight until the morning. I feel sleepy. I think I'll retire.' Then he added, smiling 'Someone is thinking "Just my luck that our paths should ever have crossed," isn't she?'

'How could I ever think such a thing? But my escort and Izumi, who are waiting for me, are no doubt feeling pretty wretched,' I answered.

'Izumi can feel wretched. Ike can feel wretched. It's not going to worry me,' he retorted, stretching out on the *tatami* mat.[84]

Then he glanced over at me. 'Oh dear! That was horrible of me. I know that you are thinking how hateful I am. What shall I do? I lay down to rest because I had a pain. Just be patient with me for a little. Ouch! how it hurts!' He laughingly carried on in this vein, making all sorts of wild exaggerations.

Such were the memories that haunted me on the way home.

48    The next morning, while I was reflecting that the carousing at the Palace was probably still going on, a very elegant letter, the fine calligraphy complemented by carefully selected paper, was sent in to me.[85] The messenger explained, 'I was told to take this to the lady, but when I arrived at the Palace, I found that she had left, and so I came here.'

While I was wondering what this was all about, the messenger added, 'It is from Lady Yamato.'[86] I opened it and read

How strong my yearning
For the palace, when I recall
The figures of the dancing maidens
Holding the emperor enthralled![87]

Hastily I wrote—

> Even at the palace there persist
> Strong memories of the past—
> Would that this rising sun might rouse him
> From eternal slumber's thrall![88]

My reply was interrupted by the excitement caused by the news that the Emperor was moving to the Koadono. Presently I left home for the Palace.[89]

I shall not describe the Great Festival of Thanksgiving, but I expect you will be able to imagine it. Everyone is familiar with the proceedings, so I shall not bother to record the details.[90]

**49** The night of the *kagura* performance arrived, and it transpired that the proceedings were no different from the *kagura* performance held in the Palace Attendants' Office.[91] Yet the performance this night did seem to be slightly more modern. Everyone looked very elegant, attired in Shinto ceremonial over-robes, decorated with red ribbons, and with white and blue braid hanging from their ceremonial caps. The flower-bedecked head-dresses reminded me of the Special Festival.[92]

Everyone took their seats, and gave their attention to their particular role. The Regent himself was conducting the choruses singing the versicles and responses, and looked splendid.[93] He was attired in formal dress, and was seated in a spot specially arranged so that he would be on a slightly higher level than everyone else. He was wearing the same flower-decked head-dress as worn by Imperial Envoys at the Special Festival—the only person present thus adorned—and looked magnificent.[94]

The Inspector Middle Counsellor, on the wooden clappers, was the chorus-leader for the versicles; his son the Middle Captain Nobumichi played the flute; while the latter's younger brother Koremichi, the Governor of Bitchū, played the cithern; and Tsunetada, the former Governor of Aki, played the flageolet. There were many others besides, but I shall not list them as it would take too long.[95]

And so the *kagura* began. The chorus leaders made such a noise with their clappers, and the voices of the singers were so resonant, as to impress even my untrained ear. Then at last the *kagura* sounded as if it were drawing to an end. When I heard the refrain, 'A thousand years, a thousand years; ten thousand years, ten thousand years,' it suddenly became obvious to me why the Goddess Amaterasu had been unable to remain concealed in her rock cave.[96]

The Gods of Ise will guard and protect our lord, who has been entrusted, at so tender an age, with the reins of the realm. His years in this great office will stretch into the distance like Nagai beach, and be as countless as the grains of sand on that shore.[97] The years of his reign will be eternal as the flow of the Mimosuso River, and as high as a mountain.[98] Surely yet another thousand generations will be added to the legendary eight-thousand generation lifespan of our precious white camellia, and during all that time the waves of the seas of the four quarters will be still.[99]

Then, as the impromptu acts following the main performance were drawing to an end, a group was made up of the Regent, who took the cithern; the Minister of Popular Affairs, Mototsuna, who took the lute; while the Middle Counsellor, Munetada, was chorus leader on the clappers as before. The reed pipes were played by the Minor Captain, Masasada, son of the Minister of the Centre; while the flute and flageolet were played by the same people as before.[1] The Regent declared, 'Let us play the tune "Ten Thousand Years",' and to his accompaniment, they played the piece through twice. This was followed by lively renditions of such pieces as *Ana tōtō* and *Ise no umi*.[2] The Middle Counsellor, Munetada, was the chorus leader on the clappers.[3]

When the performance was over, all the participants changed their clothes. The notes the Regent had drawn from his cithern, and his skilful handling of the plectrum, had been splendid. Everyone left their seats, their gift robes over their shoulders, but the Regent had received more robes than anyone else. The sight of him, with his under-robes and formal Court robes slung over his shoulder, made me think of the full moon rising over Mt Mikasa, and shedding its radiance down through the ages.[4] I felt that he was in the prime of his life, just like the cherry tree in full bloom. His glorious apparel called to mind the Wheel-Rolling King.[5] As he was leaving his seat, he said, 'These robes are gifts from His Majesty. I cannot go away leaving them here on my seat. That would be disrespectful.' So he moved off with the robes slung from his shoulder, and when he was abreast of the Imperial Throne, he said to his son, the Middle Captain, 'Come here. Take these.' He handed the robes over to his son.[6] I decided henceforth to look upon him as my protector, for it seemed that he was destined to prosper like the legendary two-leafed pine, which flourished for a thousand generations, and that this destiny would accompany him through the clouds into the next world.[7]

When the performances were over, a carriage was made ready, and I left without further ado.

50    The following day I still felt bemused by the events of the previous night, but although they had made an indelible impression on me, my thoughts were still concentrated on the late Emperor.[8] Accordingly, I sent the following poem to Suō no naishi's place, as I felt she would be able to sympathise with my feelings, having herself served more than one Emperor—

> Not for me the brilliance
> Of this splendid First Fruits Festival—
> I yearn rather for
> My accustomed cloud-palace.

She replied—

> Though absent in body
> I am with you in spirit,
> My sleeve drenched with tears—
> Yet no clouds mar the brilliance
> Of this First Fruits Festival.[9]

51    The end of the year was upon us, and I was requested by Retired Emperor Shirakawa to attend to the serving of the Emperor's meals on New Year's Day. My attendants all busied themselves with the necessary preparations, but I could not get out of my head the lines—

That last parting would slip
Yet deeper into the past.[10]

On New Year's Eve I set out for the Palace. As I passed the Horikawa Palace, Second Avenue and Horikawa Road were quite deserted, with no trace of people scurrying to and fro about their business. The sight held me fascinated, and I recalled the old poem—

There is nobody to answer
'The master is not in,'
But the state of the dwelling
Tells its own tale.[11]

52    Those who happen to read this may well be critical, and say 'It is unpleasant to find a mere lady-in-waiting giving herself such knowledgeable airs.' However, even in the case of the discussions on the Buddhist sutras, this was the sort of topic the late Emperor had been wont to bring up for my edification during the course of our conversations on various matters. I have just described things as I remember them. Nobody should be critical of that. This will all seem of no consequence to those who do not cherish the memory of the late Emperor. However, I felt so unworthy of, and so lost without, the tenderness of my late master the Emperor—one might have expected such attentions from a mistress —that I just had to record it so that it would live on in people's minds and never be forgotten.

Should the New Year catch me
Still lamenting the Emperor,
That last parting would slip
Yet deeper into the past.[12]

53    About the middle of the tenth month, l was at home, and in spite of everything, I yearned more than ever for the late Emperor, and wished he were still alive. I decided to visit the Kōryūji because, even though one could not hope to see him there, it was after all his resting place.[13]

When I arrived there, the topmost branches of all the trees had taken on their autumn tonings. The colourings seemed more intense than elsewhere—

> So wondrously intense are the colours
> Of these autumn leaves—
> Could they have been dyed by tears of blood
> Shed in longing for the past?[14]

When I approached the burial place, the pampas grasses were white-plumed and ripe, and seemed to be beckoning me, but the atmosphere of the place on the whole was unnervingly desolate rather than rosy and inviting.

'How men and women once vied in their attentions on you, and now you stand here alone and beckoning, without a single close attendant, at the foot of this distant mountain, where nobody stops by,' I thought, and was choked by such a flood of tears, that I could not even see these comfortless relics for the thick mist before my eyes—

> The pampas grasses beckon,
> Unheeded by passers-by—
> For here is only a relic,
> The substance as smoke ascended.

> How sad indeed to see
> The beckoning pampas grasses,
> Which seem to know the secrets
> Locked in the seeker's heart.

> How pitiful the tale
> Of the beckoning pampas grasses—
> Rousing sympathy in the heart
> Of one who has not seen them.

This last poem was sent to me by a certain person.[15]

54

> How were you able to record
> So pitiful a tale?
> Merely to read it overwhelms
> With uncontrollable grief.

I replied—

> I pray your sympathy—
> How distressing now I find
> This very record that I wrote
> In an attempt to console myself.[16]

## Epilogue

**55** I pondered on how I would like to show this record to someone who shared my feelings about Emperor Horikawa, if there were such a person. Everyone remembered the late Emperor with affection, but if I were to show this to someone who did not think well of me, the contents might create a furore if noised abroad, and that would be unfortunate. Then again, it would be a shame to show it to someone who was well-disposed towards me, but had neither friends nor influence. I needed somebody who fulfilled these three conditions, I decided, and concluded that Lady Hitachi alone was the one who could fulfil these three conditions.[17] I sent a carriage to collect her, and, as I had anticipated, she was delighted to come, and was completely at ease. We read to each other all day, and were still engrossed when darkness fell.

# NOTES TO THE TRANSLATION OF
## SANUKI NO SUKE NIKKI

1. It seems that Nagako began writing in the fifth month (*satsuki*) of an unspecified year—possibly 1109 or 1110. The fifth month was renowned for its
   early summer rains, giving rise to the term *samidare*, or fifth month rain.
   Nagako's reference to the skirt-hems of the peasants (*tago no mosuso*) is linked
   to these rains. Compare, for example, the poem by Lady Ise no Ōsuke
   (*Shinkokinshū*, no. 227): *Ika bakari | Tago no mosuso mo | Sobotsuramu | Kumoma
   mo mienu | Koro no samidare.*

   > Still no break in the clouds
   > Of these early summer rains—
   > How drenched will be
   > The skirts of the peasants!

2. 'The clouded vault' (*kumoi no sora*) is probably a reference to this poem in
   Book 2 of *Izumi Shikibu Shū*: *Hakanakute | Keburi to narishi | Hito ni yori |
   Kumoi no sora no | Mutsumajiki ka na.*

   > How dear to me the clouded vault
   > Where dwells the one
   > Who rose, fast smoke-transformed,
   > Into the sky.

3. The fifth day of the fifth month was the Iris Festival (*tango, ayame no sekku*).
   It was regarded as an inauspicious day, and hence many of the festival observances were aimed at warding off evil spirits. The eaves of buildings were
   covered with iris leaves, irises were worn in the hair, and in court head-dresses,
   and almost all objects of daily use were decorated.

   The phrase 'the raindrops falling on the irises decorating the eaves' (*noki no
   ayame no shizuku*) may be a reference to this poem by Tachibana no Toshitsuna
   in the Summer Section of the *Goshūishū*. *Tsurezure to | Oto taesenu wa | Samidare
   no | Noki no ayame no | Shizuku narikeri.*

   > That monotonous and constant sound
   > Is the early summer raindrops
   > Falling on the irises
   > Decorating the eaves.

4. The *hototogisu*, often translated as 'cuckoo', was credited with being able to
   cross the mountain of death (*shide no yama*). Compare the following poem by

Ise no Ōsuke from the Grief Section of the *Shūishū*: *Shide no yama | Koete kitsuramu | Hototogisu | Koishiki hito no | Ue kataramu.*

> Tell me all about
> My loved one,
> When you return
> Across the mountain of death,
> Oh, hototogisu.

No translation can do justice to the colourful combination of the pivot-word (*kakikotoba*) *sugimote*, and the pillow-word (*makura kotoba*) *isonokami* found in the phrase *sugimote isonokami furinishi mukashi*. The Isonokami Shrine is located in the Furu region of Tamba city in the Yamabe district of Nara prefecture. Since the name Furu has the associations of old, to rain, to wave or shake, it became very popular in puns.

5. My lord (*waga kimi*) is a reference to Emperor Horikawa, 73rd Emperor of Japan, who reigned from 1086 to 1107.

6. After his morning ablutions the Emperor would pray to the Ise Shrine (dedicated to the Imperial ancestress the Sun Goddess Amaterasu), and to the Sacred Mirror, before the limestone altar (*ishibai no dan*), which was located in the southern corner of the eastern ante-room of the Seiryōden. The Emperor would be attended at this time, referred to here as *ashita no onokonai*, by an Assistant Attendant (*naishi no suke*) from the Palace Attendants' Office.

7. The words 'in an attempt to console myself' (*nagusamù ya*) take on an added significance when one finds them reiterated in the last poem of the work.

8. Mount Obasute (The Mount of the Forsaken Woman) is in the district of Sarashina in Nagano prefecture. It is much famed in legend as a spot where old women who had outlived their usefulness were abandoned to die. Nagako's choice of the phrase 'as inconsolable as those who gazed on Mount Obasute' (*Obasute yama ni nagusame-kanerarete*) indicates that she had in mind this poem from the Miscellaneous Section of the *Kokinshū* (poem no. 878): *Waga kokoro | Nagusame—kanetsu | Sarashina ya | Obasute yama ni | Teru tsuki wo mite.*

> My heart finds no consolation
> At the sight of the moon
> Shining on Mount Obasute
> In Sarashina.

9. The *Chūyūki* (20–6–1107) has the following entry: 'During the night the Emperor developed a bad cold. Nevertheless, there is no cause for concern.'

10. Emperor Horikawa died in office, and the abdication ceremony was performed posthumously on the day of his death.

11. Such ladies were called *jōrō*, a term normally used in reference to Assistant Attendants (*naishi no suke*) in the Palace Attendants' Office, who held second or third rank. They were usually the daughters or grand-daughters of Ministers, and were allowed to wear the forbidden colours of purple-red (*akairo*) and

yellowish-green (*aoiro*). The identity of these particular women is not known, though the one referred to as giving birth to a child may have been the Assistant Attendant Muneko, who in 1107 gave birth to a son, Ienari, by Fujiwara no Ieyasu.

12. It was normal for an Emperor to have two or three Imperial Nurses or wet-nurses (*on-menoto*), but Horikawa had four. A very close relationship existed between an Emperor and his nurses, who were generally chosen from client families (*kinshin*) of the imperial house.

Tōzammi was Nagako's elder sister, Fujiwara no Kaneko.

Ben no sammi was Fujiwara no Mitsuko, a wife of the Major Counsellor Fujiwara no Kinzane, and mother of Michisue and Saneyoshi. She took over the upbringing of the Crown Prince, the future Emperor Toba, on the death of his mother, Fujiwara no Shishi, on 25-1-1103, only days after the baby's birth on 16-1-1103. One of the daughters, Saneko, became Toba's nurse, while another daughter, Tamako, became his consort, and mother of the future Emperors Sutoku and Go-Shirakawa.

Ōidono no sammi was Motoko, wife of the Minister of the Centre, Minamoto no Masazane. Her name is actually omitted from the text, but I have followed Tamai in including it. This inclusion can be justified on the grounds that Nagako mentions three people, and that Ōidono no sammi is present in later descriptions. The discrepancy may have resulted from a copyist's error arising from the similarity between the characters for the two names, Ōidono no sammi and Daini no sammi.

Daini no sammi was Ieko, wife of Fujiwara no Ienori, and mother of the governor of Harima, Fujiwara no Mototaka, and the governor of Izumo, Fujiwara no Ieyasu. It appears that Daini no sammi Ieko was one and the same person with Hitachi no suke Fusako, both names deriving from that of the father, Fujiwara no Iefusa, vice-governor of Hitachi.

13. Horikawa's father, Emperor Shirakawa, reigned from 1072 to 1086, and then formed his own cloister government, which he headed until his death in 1129. At this time he was residing at the Ōidono Palace.

14. The Northern Palace (Kita no In) was the residence of the Former High Priestess of the Kamo Shrines (*Saki no Saiin*), Princess Yoshiko, Horikawa's elder sister. Horikawa was presently residing at the Horikawa Palace, and his sister lived immediately to the north of this. The *Chūyūki* records (6-7-1107) that the Retired Emperor moved hurriedly to the residence of the Former High Priestess of the Kamo Shrines and installed himself in the Western Wing.

15. The Minister of the Centre (*Naidaijin*) was Minamoto no Masazane, younger brother of Horikawa's mother, Katako, and consequently Horikawa's uncle. While Katako was the daughter of Minamoto no Akifusa, she had been adopted by a former Regent, Fujiwara no Morozane. The Regent at this time was Fujiwara no Tadazane. He currently held the positions of Minister of the Right

(*Udaijin*) and Chancellor (*kampaku*). As he became Regent (*sesshō*) on Horikawa's death, I have preferred to refer to him throughout as Regent, in order to avoid confusion.

16. Archbishop Zōyo was High Priest of the Tendai sect of Buddhism, Archbishop of Miidera, and Horikawa's religious mentor. At this time he was aged 76. He is best remembered for his popularisation of *Shugendō*, a school of Buddhism, the aim of which was not to study doctrines, but to undergo religious exercises in the mountains. Zōyo founded the *Shōgoin-ryū*, also called the Honzan School, of the Tendai branch of *Shugendō*. The titles *sōjō* (Archbishop), *sōzu* (Bishop) and *risshi* (Master of Asceticism) were the three major positions in the *sōgō* system of Buddhist ranks. Raiki and Zōken were both priests from Miidera, aged 58 and 32 respectively.

17. It was believed that, through prayer, the evil spirit causing a disease would be transferred to a medium, and would reveal its identity and what was troubling it.

18. A curtain of state (*kichō*) would have been erected beside the Emperor when Raiki arrived.

19. In this passage Horikawa is apparently referring to the arrangements necessary for his abdication.

The *sonshō* (abbreviation of *sonshōhō*) was a type of ritual (*shuhō*) found especially in esoteric Buddhism, and which took as its object of worship the *butchōson*, or deified form of the lump (*usnīsa*) on the crown of Buddha's head. The ritual of burning (*goma*) originated with fire-worshipping *brāhmans* who thought that fire was the mouth of heaven and that, if they made offerings to the fire, heaven would give benefits to man. Esoteric Buddhists adopted this method. They made a fire with wood, so that this fire, symbolising wisdom, might burn defilements and dissipate the curses of devils. A special type of altar known as *gomadan* or *rodan* was used, in which a furnace was placed inside an altar.

There are various types of confession (*sembō*), but two typical forms are confession after seeing the truth, and confession after worship, sutra-chanting, etc. The term can also refer to confession through reciting the *Anraku gyōbon* of the *Hokekō* (*Lotus Sutra*).

I have followed Ishii Fumio's suggestions in translating this passage. There is some discrepancy between texts, and this passage might be translated 'The ritual of burning must be performed at nine altars, and the confession of sins be made, at the Sonshōji which I built.' This temple was built by order of Horikawa, and dedicated on 21-7-1102.

20. This is possibly a reference to the provision of nine altars. Usually five was the limit.

21. This robe was a *nōshi* or *naoshi*, the 'ordinary' Court cloak, which was a voluminous wide-sleeved gown worn by men.

22. The Crown Prince Munehito was aged five at the time of Horikawa's death.

23. The term *nageshi*, translated in this passage as threshold, refers to the transverse beams at the top and bottom of a threshold, separating the *hisashi* (ante-room) from the *moya* (main part of the room). The beams referred to in this work are generally those at the bottom of the threshold, or *shimonageshi*.

24. The sender of this message was Nagako's elder sister, Tōzammi.

25. The Sacred Jewel (*shinji*), also known as the *Yasakani no magatama* was one of the Three Sacred Treasures symbolising the Emperor's authority. The jewel was kept in a box, which was placed on a shelf near the Emperor's pillow, on the eastern side of the dais in the bedchamber. The Sacred Sword (*Ame no murakumo no tsurugi*) was also kept on this shelf.

26. *Hiru* or *nobiru—Allium nipponicum*; a variety of wild garlic, the leaves and stalk of which were boiled.

27. About 6 a.m. the garden in front of the Palace was swept by workers from the Office of Grounds (*tonomori zukasa*).

28. Wooden latticed shutters or gratings (*kōshi*) divided the *sunoko* (open verandah) from the *hisashi* (ante-room). The shutters were lacquered black, and had a white lining on the inside. It was normal for there to be two shutters, an upper and a lower, between each set of pillars. The lower one was removable, while the upper one would be hooked up to the roof during the day. The shutters were put up at 7 a.m. by a Chamberlain (*kurōdo*). When the shutters were raised, a woman from the Office of Grounds would lower the oil-lamps.

29. This person was probably one of Nagako's own attendants, perhaps the Izumi who appears later.

30. According to the *Denreki* and *Chūyūki*, Horikawa was sick in the 3rd, 7th, 8th, 9th and 10th months of 1105.

31. The episode of the Emperor hiding Nagako behind his knees made a profound impression on her, and she mentions the incident three times in her diary. According to her account, it would seem that the incident occurred on the 15th day, but the *Chūyūki* and *Denreki* indicate it occurred on the 10th or 11th days.

32. *Denreki* (17-7-1107) records that seven images of the Healing Buddha (Yakushibotoke) were constructed, and ceremonies commenced before them. *Chūyūki* (14-7-1107) records that it was determined that 1000 priests would begin chanting the sutras on the nineteenth day.

33. The term envoy (*senji*) originally referred to a woman official who transmitted the Emperor's words to the Chamberlains (*kurōdo*), and who acted as a general go-between. Later it was permissible for the Empress, Crown Prince, High Priestess of the Kamo Shrines, Chancellor and Regent to have in their service a high-ranking lady-in-waiting who transmitted their words to others.

　　The Empress (*chūgū*), Atsuko, was a sister of Shirakawa, and consequently Horikawa's aunt. She had come to court as a *nyōgo* in 1091, aged 32, and in

1093 was made *chūgū*. No children resulted from the union. The titles of imperial consorts were—First Empress (*kōgō*), Second Empress (*chūgū*), Imperial Lady (*nyōgo*), Imperial Concubine (*kōi*). At this time, Atsuko was residing in the Eastern Wing (*higashi no tai*) of the Horikawa Palace.

The Sammi in question is probably Nagako's elder sister, Tōzammi. There seems to have been some distant relationship between the Empress Atsuko, Tōzammi and Nagako, probably through somebody now deceased.

34. Ice was brought to the Palace from the iceworks north of Kyoto. In the *Nihonshoki* there is a mention of iceworks being in existence in the reign of Emperor Nintoku (313?–399). After the Taika Reforms the iceworks came under the control of the *mondo no tsukasa*. At the Ice Festival (*himuro no sechie*), ice was brought to the Palace on the first day of the sixth month and distributed to the assembled nobles. Horikawa seems to have been repeating this performance for fun.

35. At the Imperial Palace, the bed-chamber (*yoru no otodo*) was situated in the main building (*omoya*) of the Seiryōden. However, the Emperor was now residing at the Horikawa Palace, where the Western Wing (*nishi no tai*) corresponded to the Seiryōden. Following the example set in 1080 when Shirakawa stayed at the Horikawa Palace, the *nurigome* (a small, walled-in room, similar to a closet) was used as the bed-chamber.

A curtain of state (*kichō*) was a type of screen consisting of two slender wooden pillars three or four *shaku* high, set in a wooden base, and supporting a transverse bar from which hung four or five drops of material (*katabira*). The gaps between these curtains were known as *hokorobi*.

36. Blinds of reed or split bamboo (*misu, sudare*) were used to separate the *hisashi* (ante-room) from the *moya* (main part of the room), or the *hisashi* from the *sunoko* (open verandah). It is this latter type which seem to be referred to here.

37. The Captain of the Outer Palace Guards of the Left (*saemon no kami*) was Horikawa's uncle, Minamoto no Masatoshi, a younger brother of the Minister of the Centre, Masazane.

The Minamoto Middle Counsellor (*Minamoto chūnagon*) was another of Horikawa's uncles, Minamoto no Kunizane, a younger brother of Masatoshi.

The Provisional Middle Counsellor (*gon-chūnagon*) was Horikawa's cousin, Minamoto no Akimichi, the son of the Minister of the Centre, Masazane. Akimichi's mother was Horikawa's nurse, Ōidono no sammi.

The Imperial Adviser and Middle Captain (*saishō no chūjō*) was Minamoto no Yoshitoshi, son of Toshiaki. *Saishō* was the Chinese term for an Imperial Adviser (*sangi*).

The Major Controller of the Left (*sadaiben*) was Minamoto no Shigesuke, son of Tsunenari.

38. The lamps were lit at dusk by women from the Office of Grounds.

39. Incantations used in esoteric Buddhism (*kaji*) involved making signs (*mudrās*)

with the hands, reciting *darani*, purifying objects, and invoking Buddha's divine protection.

40. *Chūyūki* (18–7–1106) records that the Emperor's body had become very swollen from the day before.

41. The Archbishop in question is probably Zōyo, though the *Chūyūki* (18–7–1107) records that Archbishop Ningen was present from the 16th day.

    The phrase 'smoke is pouring from his ears' (*kashira yori kuro-keburi wo tatete*) seems to have been an idiomatic expression.

42. These events occurred on the eighteenth day of the seventh month.

43. *Denreki* records that on the 16th and 17th days the Abbot of the Enryakuji, Archbishop Ningen, who was the 40th patriarch of the Tendai sect, performed Buddhist rituals before seven statues of the Healing Buddha (Yakushi), assisted on the 17th day by other priests. *Chūyūki* (18–7–1107) records that Ningen had been performing rituals before the seven statues of the Healing Buddha since the 16th day, and on the 18th led the multitude in the Central Hall in prayers and incantations.

44. Gyōson was a famous mountain ascetic. He was the son of Minamoto no Motohira, and lived from 1057–1135. He entered the priesthood at the age of 12, and became Archbishop (*dai-sōjō*) of Miidera. In the Hōan era (1120–1123) he became Chief Abbot (*zasu*) of the Tendai sect, at the Enryakuji. He also became Emperor Toba's religious mentor. He was skilled at poetry. Miidera, or the Onjōji, was the head temple of the Tendai-jimon sect. It is situated in Shiga prefecture.

45. *Senjukyō* is an abbreviation for *Senju sengen kanzeon bosatsu kōdai emman muge daihishin darani kyō*. This sutra recounts the virtues of the Kannon of the one thousand arms and eyes, who is supposed to take an especial interest in hungry spirits and ghosts. The line quoted is a line from a verse in the middle of the sutra.

46. Archbishop Ryū may be Ryūmyō, son of Fujiwara no Takaie. He had been Archbishop (*daisōjō*) at Miidera for many years, and died on 14–9–1104.

    Raigō was a Holy Teacher (*ajari*) at Miidera. He had prayed successfully for the birth of Shirakawa's first son, Atsufumi, but, incensed at Shirakawa's refusal to reward him with the establishment of an ordination platform at Miidera, had fasted to death on 4–5–1084, and uttered a curse which was supposed to have caused Atsufumi's death.

47. As both Ryūmyō and Raigō came from Miidera, this is presumably the temple in question. However, there is no record of Horikawa ever having visited Miidera.

48. The ceremony referred to here is the *jukai*, a Buddhist confirmation service at which the Buddhist Precepts were acknowledged, usually in the presence of three leaders and seven witnesses.

    The *Chūyūki* (18–7–1107) states that the Master of the Buddhist Law (*sensei hōin*) in question was Kensen. He was the son of Minamoto no Nobuyori, was abbot (*zasu*) of the Hōshōji, and became 41st patriarch of the Tendai sect. At this time he was aged 79, and was Horikawa's religious mentor. *Hōin* is the highest rank in the *sōi* hierarchal system. This was a system of hierarchal ranking awarded by the Court according to the degree of learning and virtue of the priest. Although the system underwent various changes, it generally centered around the three ranks of *hōin*, *hōgen* and *hokkyō*, which corresponded to the three *sōgō* ranks of *sōjō*, *sōzu* and *risshi*.

49. *Denreki* (18–7–1107) records that the ceremony took place about 10 p.m.

50. The Assistant Attendant (*suke*) in question is apparently Nagako.

51. The gong referred to here is a *kei*, a type of gong sounded before an image of Buddha, and usually consisting of a piece of copper in the shape of a shallow inverted 'V', suspended from a frame.

The chapel (*futama*) was a room in which a statue of Buddha was enshrined, and where the priest on duty prayed for the health and well-being of the Emperor. In the Seiryōden, this room was situated just off the bed-chamber, in the *higashi-bisashi* (eastern ante-room).

52. The Emperor's robe differed from the ordinary *nōshi* in that it had a long train, and was known thus as a *hikinōshi*. With it was worn a ceremonial cap (*kōburi*), and a scarlet long divided skirt (*naga-hakama*). At the neck of the *nōshi* was a fastening (*himo*) consisting of a jewelled toggle on the left, and a loop on the right.

53. Before the confirmation ceremony began, it was the procedure for the officiating priest to read a prose passage explaining the purpose of the ceremony. The passage quoted here fulfils this purpose, and in its original form would have been written in *kambun*.

The Ten Buddhist Precepts or rules of discipline (*jikkai*) concern the self-discipline required to perform the ten good deeds (*jūzen*)—(1) not to kill, (2) not to steal, (3) not to commit adultery, (4) not to lie, (5) not to use immoral language, (6) not to slander, (7) not to equivocate, (8) not to covet, (9) not to give way to anger, (10) not to hold false views.

The reward for observing the Ten Precepts was rebirth in one of the heavens, or rebirth among men, depending on the degree of observance (*jūzen no i*). This term was often applied to the attainment of the position of Emperor as a reward for observing the Precepts.

54. The order of ceremony was that the officiating priest would read out each Precept and ask 'Do you swear to abide by this?', to which the candidate would reply 'I swear to abide by this'.

55. Jōkai was the son of Minamoto no Akifusa, and was one of Horikawa's uncles. At this time he was aged 33. *Azari* or *ajari* (*ācārya*) was a distinguished title given to learned priests of the Tendai and Shingon sects.

56. The *Lotus Sutra* (*Hokekyō* or *Myōhō-renge-kyō*, Sanskrit, *Saddharmapundarīka-*

*sutra*) is the main text of the Tendai and Nichiren sects of Buddhism. Although it is one of the most important sutras of Mahāyāna Buddhism, it teaches that even followers of Hīnayāna Buddhism are able to attain perfect enlightenment, and that this had been achieved by Buddha many ages ago.

The sutra contains eight books (*kan*), each subdivided into two to five chapters (*hon*), making twenty-eight chapters in all. The chapter, 'On Tactfulness' (*Hōbenbon*), is the second chapter of the first book.

The sutra combines both prose passages (*jōgō*) and verse passages (*ge*). In the chapter, 'On Tactfulness', is a verse, part of which is as follows:

> *Bhikshus* and *bhikshunīs*
> Obsessed by utmost arrogance,
> *Upāsikās* (filled with) self-conceit,
> *Upāsakās* with unbelief,
> Four groups such as these,
> Five thousand in number,
> Perceiving not their errors
> And faults in the commandments,
> Careful only of their flaws,
> Such small wit they showed,
> These dregs of the assembly, who
> Because of the Buddha's splendid virtue withdrew;
> These men of little virtuous happiness
> Are incapable of receiving this Law.

(See Katō Bunnō (trans.), *Myōhō-Renge-Kyō, The Sutra of the Lotus Flower of the Wonderful Law*, revised by W. E. Soothill and Wilhelm Schiffer, 1971), p. 48.

*Bhikshu* (Japanese *biku*) refers to a Buddhist monk or mendicant while *bhikshunī* (Japanese *bikuni*) refers to a Buddhist nun or female mendicant.

57. The Sammi in question seems to be Tōzammi, Nagako's elder sister.

58. This passage is rather garbled, and my attempt at translation is based largely on Ishii.

59. The *Kannonbon* or *Kanzeon bosatsu fumonbon* (*The Chapter on the Samantamukha of Avalokiteśvara*) is the 25th chapter, in Book 8, of the *Lotus Sutra*. It is commonly known as the *Kannongyō* or *Kannon sutra*. The work says that anyone uttering the name of Kannon will be saved from all calamities of shipwreck, fire or moral impurity. It is said that Kannon takes the form of the beings he is to save, and delivers them from all trouble.

60. Towards the end of Chapter 25 there is a long verse in praise of Kannon, the Bodhisattva Regarder-of-the-Cries-of-the-World. The verse ends

> Regarder of the World's Cries, pure and holy,
> In pain, distress, death, calamity,
> Able to be a sure reliance,

Perfect in all merit,
With compassionate eyes beholding all,
Boundless oceans of blessings!
Prostrate let us revere him.

See Katō, p. 414.

61. Michinokuni paper was thick, white paper used for writing notes, love letters, etc. and normally carried tucked inside one's robe. It was manufactured in the district of Michinoku(ni) in the north of the main island. Originally the bark of the spindle-tree was used, but later the mulberry.

62. *Denreki* and *Chūyūki* both record that the Emperor's condition worsened about 6 a.m. on the 19th day.

63. The invocation *Namu Amida Butsu* was the most usual formula of the Pure Land *nembutsu*, the invocation of the name of Amida (Amitabha), the Buddha of Infinite Life. Amida was the ruler of the Western Paradise, and it was held that he came to the deathbed to welcome to his Pure Land those believers who called on his name.

64. The *Daihannya sutra* or Great Wisdom Sutra (Japanese *Daihannyakyō, Daihannya haramittakyō*, Sanskrit *Mahāprajñāpāramitā sūtra*) is a long work setting forth the doctrine of *sūnyatā* or relativity. According to the *Chūyūki*, Horikawa had been copying it over a period of years.

65. The Ise Shrine (*Daijingū*) is the shrine at which Amaterasu Ōmikami, the ancestress of the imperial family, is worshipped. It is situated at Ise, in Mie prefecture.

66. This invocation (Japanese *namu byōdō daie kō myōhōke*) corresponds to the more familiar invocation *namu myōhō renge kyō*, the invocation of the *Lotus Sutra* advocated by the Nichiren sect as the means of attaining salvation.

67. The Archbishop in question was Archbishop Zōyo.

*Denreki* (19-7-1107) records how the Regent hurriedly appeared on hearing of the Emperor's deteriorating condition, and how he summoned those priests engaged in rituals (*shuhō*) and those engaged in reading the sutras.

68. This is a reference to *mappō*, or the Latter Stages of the Law. There was a belief that the Buddhist Law would go through three stages, and that the final stage would see the decay of the Law. This final stage was predicted to begin in 1052.

69. *Denreki* (19-7-1107) records that the Emperor died about 8 a.m. uttering the *nembutsu* and invoking the sacred names of sutras.

70. The Minister of Popular Affairs (*mimbu no kyō*) was Minamoto no Toshiaki, son of Takakuni, and father of the *saishō no chūjō* Yoshitoshi.

*Denreki* (19-7-1107) records that about 1 p.m. the Minister of Popular Affairs was sent to report the Emperor's death to the Retired Emperor, and to mention the matter of the succession.

71. This was probably the address to the departed soul, explaining how to travel safely through the underworld.

72. *Chūyūki* (19–7–1107) states that the Archbishop left at 1 p.m.
73. High Court Noble (*kandachime* or *kandachibe*) was a designation for all gentle-men of third rank and above, and for Imperial Advisers (*sangi*) of the fourth rank, but not usually applied to the Chancellor or Regent.

   Senior Courtier (*tenjōbito*) was a designation for gentlemen of the fourth or fifth rank who had the privilege of waiting in attendance on the Emperor in the Senior Courtiers' Chamber (*tenjō no ma*). Sometimes gentlemen of sixth rank would be included in this category.
74. *Denreki* (19–7–1107) says the priests left about 10 a.m., but the *Chūyūki* entry for the same day records that the priests performing *shuhō* and reading sutras gradually dispersed after the Archbishop left at 1 p.m.
75. This was Ningen, son of Fujiwara no Morozane, and uncle of the Regent, Tadazane.
76. Apparently Nagako's elder sister, Tōzammi, had been assisted to the Emperor's chamber by some of her own attendants, who had had to leave her at the entrance, since they were not allowed in the Emperor's presence. Tōzammi was clad in a *karaginu*, or short, formal 'Chinese' jacket, worn over, and in a contrasting colour to, the long, flowing robe (*uchigi*). A *karaginu* was sleeve-length in front, but shorter at the back. The colour of this *karaginu* was *futaai*, a violet colour produced by mixing blue and scarlet.
77. Akikuni was the son of Minamoto no Kunizane. He was Horikawa's younger cousin, and at this time was aged 25.

   Iesada was the son of Minamoto no Akifusa. He was Horikawa's uncle, and at this time was aged 29. He later changed his name to Nobumasa.
78. When an Emperor died, the normal procedure was for his head to be laid to the north, his clothes changed and the body covered, the mats (*tatami*) to be replaced by straw mats (*mushiro*), paper sliding-screens erected round the bed and lamps lit beside the pillow. When death took place on the *tatami*, the cover was cut off and the padding removed.
79. The Governor of Harima was Fujiwara no Mototaka. His younger brother, Ieyasu, was Governor of Izumo. Both were sons born to Fujiwara no Ienori by Daini no sammi Ieko. Ieyasu may have been Horikawa's foster-brother.
80. This was Atsukane, the son born to Fujiwara no Atsuie and Tōzammi Kaneko. Atsukane was one of Horikawa's foster-brothers.
81. It is hard to determine the speakers in the preceding conversation. I have followed Ishii's interpretation.
82. This was Koreko, the daughter of Fujiwara no Koretsune. She was a Junior Assistant (*naishi no jō*) in the Palace Attendants' Office, and a great favourite of Horikawa. *Chūyūki* (24–7–1107) records that she was one of the Junior Assistants permitted to wear mourning.
83. The Daytime Chamber (*hi no omashi*) normally referred to the main room (*moya*) of the Seiryōden, and was situated to the south of the bed-chamber

(*yoru no otodo*). The curtain-dais (*michōdai*) was situated to the north of the centre of the Daytime Chamber, and facing east. Beside this were placed the statues of a leonine creature known as *shishi* and of a 'Korean' dog (*komainu*), which were supposed to ward off evil influences. On the southern side of the curtain-dais were three dining-tables about four by two feet and one foot high (*daishōji*), and to the south of them again were two small cupboards (*zushi*). Within the curtain-dais a mirror (*mikagami*) hung from two pillars on the western side. In the Horikawa Palace the Daytime Chamber was situated in the main room of the Western Wing, to the south of the bed-chamber.

*Denreki* (19–7–1107) records 'At about 8 p.m. I [the Regent] and the Minister of the Centre went to the bed-chamber. I waited outside while the Minister of the Centre fetched the Sacred Jewel, Sacred Sword, etc. . . . I was in front of the curtain-dais and took them and placed them inside the curtain-dais in the Daytime Chamber.' Included also is an 'inventory of items moved tonight' which lists 'the mace box, 3 dining-tables from the Daytime Chamber, two small cupboards, two leonine statues, the seats for the Senior Courtiers, the time board, and the shelf where Imperial meals were served'.

The Sacred Jewel, Sacred Sword, etc., had to be moved to the Ōidono, where the Crown Prince, Munehito, was residing.

84. This was Takashina no Nariko, who served as a Junior Assistant in the Palace Attendants' Office during the reigns of Horikawa and Toba.

85. The Imperial Dining Room (*asagarei no omashi* or *asagarei no ma*) was a room in the western ante-room of the Seiryōden where ceremonial meals were served to the Emperor in the mornings and evenings; his real meals were eaten elsewhere. This function was performed by Assistant Attendants, who were permitted into the northern part of the room, and by Junior Assistants, who remained outside the paper sliding-door. Apparently Nagako had never performed this function.

The events described in this section antedate the previous section. This and the somewhat disjointed narrative would seem to indicate that it belonged to a larger section, now lost.

86. Nagako received Retired Emperor Shirakawa's request to return to court to serve Emperor Toba in the tenth month of 1107. The request was transmitted to her by Toba's nurse, Ben no sammi, also known as Fujiwara no Mitsuko.

87. This poem (*Ama no kawa | Onaji nagare to | Kikinagara | Wataran koto wa | Nao zo kanashiki*) occurs in the Miscellaneous section of the *Goshūishū*, and is prefaced by the words—'Written on receiving a message from the recently enthroned Emperor Go-Sanjō, ordering me to go to the Palace on the seventh day of the seventh month. At the time I was in retirement at home, reflecting in a confused way over the sorrowfulness of life in this world.'

Its authoress, Suō no naishi, was a famous poetess, who served initially as a Junior Assistant at the court of Emperor Go-Reizei (died 19–4–1068), returned to hold the same position at the court of Emperor Shirakawa, and later attended Emperors Horikawa and Toba. She was the daughter of the Govenor of Suō, Taira no Munenaka.

Since she was requested to attend court on the seventh day of the seventh month, which was the day of the Weaver Festival (*tanabata matsuri*), she employed in her poem imagery connected with the festival. The poem contains a double meaning through the use of three *engo*—words with associated meanings.

(a) *ama no kawa*—the River of Heaven or Milky Way—is used in the sense of the Emperor.

(b) *nagare*—stream—is used in the sense of line, blood, ancestry, and refers to the fact that Go-Sanjō is the younger brother of the late Go-Reizei.

(c) *wataru*—to cross—is used in the sense of to serve, to attend.

The implied meaning of the poem is therefore—Although I know that the new Emperor is of the same line as the old, I am still sorrowful at being asked to serve him.

88. The phrase 'as deranged as the seaweed gathered by the fishermen' (*ama no karu mo ni omoimidareshika*) is a reference to an anonymous poem in the Miscellaneous section of the *Kokinshū* (poem no. 934): *Iku yo shimo | Araji waga mi wo | Nazo mo kaku | Ama no karu mo ni | Omoimidaruru.*

> Why am I so deranged,
> When I, like the seaweed
> Gathered by the fishermen,
> Have so short a time left to live?

89. Emperor Toba's nurses were Ben no sammi (Fujiwara no Mitsuko), Dainagon no suke (Fujiwara no Saneko), and Ben no suke (Fujiwara no Yoshiko). Ben no sammi was promoted to third rank in 1102, while the two latter were appointed as Assistant Attendants on 26–10–1107, on which occasion Saneko was elevated to Junior Fifth Rank Lower Grade, which rank Yoshiko already held. The letter therefore rather exaggerated the situation.

The *Kimpishō* states that only Assistant Attendants or noblewomen permitted to wear the forbidden colours could serve the Emperor's meals. Assistant Attendants were appointed from those of fifth rank or over.

90. This poem (*Kawaku ma mo | Naki kurozome no | Tamoto kana | Aware mukashi no | Katami to omou ni*) is based on one written by Nagako's father, Akitsuna, on the death of Emperor Go-Sanjō: (*Kawaku ma mo | Naki kurozome no | Tamoto kana | Kuchinaba nani wo | Katami to mo semu*)

> Ah, this dear black sleeve
> Drenched though it be with tears—
> What would I have as a keepsake
> Were it to rot away?

*Tamoto* actually refers to that section of the close-fitting mourning robe between the shoulder and elbow, but is used also of the sleeve in general.

91. Emperor Toba's accession ceremony (*onsokui*) was held on 1–12–1107.

92. Imperial Nurse Dainagon was Saneko, daughter of the Major Counsellor, Fujiwara no Kinzane, and Ben no sammi (see note 12). She was the wife of the former Governor of Aki, Tsunetada. She was appointed as one of the court ladies to perform the duty of opening and closing the curtains around the throne at the accession ceremony (*tobariage* or *kenchō*). However, she was prevented from so doing by the death of her father, Kinzane, after a long illness, on 14–11–1107.

   *Tenso reiki shokushō roku* records that Fujiwara no Kaneko was in charge of the right-hand curtains at the accession of Emperor Horikawa.

93. The Director of the Palace Treasury (*kura no kō no tono*) was Fujiwara no Tamefusa. The Palace Treasury (*kuraryō*) was a bureau under the Ministry of Central Affairs (*nakazukasa shō*). Tamefusa also held at this time the similar sounding title of Chief Chamberlain (*kurōdo no tō*). This post was the highest in the Emperor's Private Office (*kurōdodokoro*), which was in charge of matters relating to the Emperor and his Palace. It was probably in this latter capacity that Tamefusa sent the imperial order (*senji*) to Nagako. This message went through the following stages of transmission: (1) Retired Emperor Shirakawa sent an order (*inzen*) to the Regent Tadazane; (2) the Regent, acting on behalf of Emperor Toba, gave an order (*senji*) to the Director of the Palace Treasury, in his capacity as Chief Chamberlain; (3) the Director of the Palace Treasury sent a messenger to Nagako; (4) someone from Nagako's household brought the message to the place where she was seeking advice.

   At the time of Horikawa's death, Shirakawa had instructed that certain nobles and palace attendants who had been close to the late Emperor be permitted to wear mourning clothes. *Chūyūki* (24–7–1107) records that Nagako was one of the ladies-in-waiting so permitted.

94. The mourning period finished on the first anniversary of Horikawa's death. The phrase 'the parsley picker referred to in an old song' (*seritsumishi to iiken furugoto*) is a reference to an old song: *Seri tsumishi | Mukashi no hito mo | Waga goto ya | Kokoro ni mono wa | Kanawazarikemu*.

> That parsley-picker of yore—
> Was he, like me,
> Unable to attain
> His heart's desire?

This song appears to be based on an old story about a low-born man who falls in love with a girl of noble rank he chances to see as she is eating wild parsley (parsley being a convenient translation for *seri* or *Oenanthe stolinifera*). He later tries to console himself by picking parsley and eating it, but this only makes him more miserable. The phrase *seri tsumu* therefore came to mean 'not to have things one's own way', or 'to be unhappy'.

95. The term foster-brother (*onmenotogo*) is used of the child an Imperial nurse was rearing at the same time as she nursed the Emperor. A very close relationship existed between the Emperor and his foster-brothers.

96. Emperor Kazan (984–986) abdicated suddenly in order to become a priest, and was succeeded by Emperor Ichijō (986–1011). The Regent at this time was Fujiwara no Kaneie, who later, on renouncing the world, took the name Hōkōin nyūdō dono. Fujiwara no Koreshige had served as Provisional Middle Controller of the Left (*Gon sachūben*) during the reign of Emperor Kazan.

There were six Controllers—a Major, Middle and Minor Controller in each of the two Controlling Boards (*Sabenkan* and *Ubenkan*). These officers were known as the *rokuza*.

97. This passage contains an interesting blend of Buddhist and Shinto belief and practice. The belief that all events in this life are rigidly predetermined by behaviour in previous existences is contained in the Buddhist term *karma*. The authoress does not actually employ this term, but she does refer to the equivalent 'bond from a previous existence' (*saki no yo no chigiri*). Then, according to Shinto ritual it was customary, at the end of a period of mourning, to purify oneself with water from the river.

98. A memorial service was held at the Horikawa Palace on the 19th day of each month, until the first anniversary of Horikawa's death.

*Chūyūki* (19-11-1107) records, 'The sky is overcast, and it is snowing. The cold wind pierces you like a sword. In the evening I went to the Horikawa Palace. This was because of the monthly anniversary.'

99. According to *Denreki* and *Chūyūki*, the ceremony usually began about 2 p.m.

1. Second Avenue (Nijō no ōji) was one of the nine great avenues (*jō*) running at equal distances across Kyoto from east to west. Being directly south of the Imperial Palace, it was the largest and most impressive, almost 60 yards wide. The Horikawa Palace took up two blocks (*chō*) at the intersection of Second Avenue and Horikawa Road, being situated on the southern side of Second Avenue and the eastern side of Horikawa Road.

2. The Daigokuden was a State Chamber (*seiden*) situated at the northern end, in the centre, of the Hasshōin, or Chōdōin, as it was also called. The Hasshōin was a government office within the Greater Imperial Palace, where the officials of the eight ministries gathered, and where the Emperor inquired into the government and gave audience. The Daigokuden contained the Imperial Throne and was the actual chamber from which the Emperor directed the government. Important ceremonies such as the New Year and accession ceremonies were held there. The roof was tiled with blue-green tiles, and on either side of the ridge poles were bronze-gilded ornamental tiles. On the

eastern and western sides at the front were two turrets—one decorated with a blue dragon, the other with a white tiger.

The Western Gate (*nishi no jin*) is probably a reference to the guardhouse at the Kōhammon, the gate on the western side of the Hasshōin, closest to the Daigokuden.

It was usual for a path of straw mats (*endō*) to be laid from the gate of a house to the main building, to prevent the hems of visitors' clothes becoming soiled.

3. Emperor Horikawa resided at the Imperial Palace from 25-9-1102 to 5-2-1104, and from 8-6-1105 to 25-2-1106.

4. The Northern Gate (*kita no mon*) probably refers to the Shōkeimon, the northern gate of the Hasshōin.

Women participants in Shinto ceremonies wore a loose white robe (*chihaya*), patterned with greyish-green butterflies or water-grasses.

5. This sentence is rather obscure. The *Denreki* account (1-12-1107) throws some light on the subject. Describing the robes to be worn in the Koadono by the ladies-in-waiting to the Empress Mother, it says that dark-red (*suō*) under-robes (*uchigi*), dark-red beaten silk over-robes (*uchiginu*), Chinese jackets (*karaginu*) of light-green woven material, and printed trains (*surimo*) were placed in a long chest and despatched for the ceremony. The syllables *suō no koki utaru* may therefore refer to the dark-red over-robes of beaten silk. When the *uchigi* was worn so that its lower edge showed beneath the divided skirt (*hakama*), it was known as *idashiuchigi* and this is probably what is meant by *idashiginu*.

6. The Imperial Sun Crow (*Yatagarasu*) was a supernatural bird with three legs which lived in the sun. It is credited with having guided Emperor Jimmu from Kumano to Yoshino. On occasions such as the accession ceremony, two rows of standards were arranged in line with the cherry tree and the orange tree in the courtyard to the south of the Shishinden. One standard was a three-legged bird of yellow-coloured copper atop a golden lotus throne on a black-lacquered shaft decorated with a cloud design in five colours. Seven streamers hung from beneath the lotus throne. This standard was known as *dōu no tō*.

To the east of the Imperial Sun Crow standard stood the Sun standard (*nichizōtō*)—a gold-lacquered dial with a representation of a three-legged red bird, surrounded by seventeen gold-lacquered skewers and atop a black-lacquered shaft which ran through nine gold-lacquered discs. Opposite stood the Moon standard (*getsuzōtō*)—similar to the Sun standard but decorated with a rabbit, toad, laurel tree and bright blue tiles.

The military banners (*ōgashira, taitō*) were cloth banners of various designs attached to a shaft which was topped by a crown of black hair from the tail of a bullock.

7. *Eiga Monogatari* is an historical tale (*rekishi monogatari*) covering the reigns from Emperor Uda to Emperor Horikawa. It concludes with the year 1092, and

bears the mark of various writers. The ladies-in-waiting, Akazome Emon, Ben no naishi and Suō no naishi, have been named as having contributed. For a long time *Eiga Monogatari* and its successors, *Ōkagami* and *Ima Kagami*, were all known as *Yotsugi*.

8. Emperor Toba had to process from the Ōidono to the Daigokuden. *Denreki* says he arrived at 10 a.m., *Chūyūki* at noon.

9. Ceremonial jewelled caps (*tama no kōburi*) were worn by civil officials of fifth rank and above on occasions when ceremonial dress was indicated. Jewels were set in a gold semi-circle around the cap. The number and colour of the jewels was determined according to rank.

Brocaded sleeveless over-robes (*uchikake*) were worn by military officials at important ceremonies over their other clothing. Major, Middle and Minor Captains of the Inner Palace Guards wore brocaded over-robes, while Lieutenants of the Inner and Outer Palace Guards wore embroidered over-robes.

The Officer of the Middle Palace Guards (*konoezukasa*) was charged with guarding the Imperial Palace and accompanying imperial processions. The Minor Captains in particular wore ceremonial armour (*yoroi*). This type of armour was usually made of silk, marked over with ink and hardened with lacquer, and was worn over the other clothes on important occasions such as accompanying an imperial procession.

10. The Assistant Captain of the Outer Palace Guards was Fujiwara no Akitaka, who also held the positions of Chamberlain and Middle Controller of the Left, and whose wife, Ben no suke, was a wet-nurse to Emperor Toba.

The Regent Tadazane records in *Denreki* (1-12-1107) how he placed Tamefusa to the left and Akitaka to the right, and how both were dressed in military ceremonial caps and ceremonial armour, and holding halberts. They therefore looked rather like Bishamon—or Bishamonten (*Vaiśravana*), one of the Four Quarter Kings (*shitennō*), who is usually depicted wearing helmet and armour. He lives in the fourth layer of Mt Sumeru, and protects people living in the northern part of the world.

11. The *Denreki* and *Chūyūki* accounts indicate that about 4 p.m. the Emperor ascended his throne from the steps at the rear. Two ladies-in-waiting mounted the steps on either side of the throne and opened the curtains. They were joined by attendants who fastened the curtains back with pins. All then retired to their seats.

12. Ben no suke was Fujiwara no Yoshiko, one of Toba's nurses, and the wife of Fujiwara no Akitaka. Ben no sammi and Dainagon no suke were the wife and daughter respectively of the late Fujiwara no Kinzane. They were unable to attend court since they were still in mourning.

13. This was New Year's Day 1108. After his accession, Emperor Toba had moved from the Ōidono to the Ko-Rokujōden.

14. This song is referred to in Chapter 181 of the *Tsurezuregusa* of Yoshida no Kaneyoshi, or Kenkō.

'The meaning of the word *koyuki* in the song, "Fure, fure, koyuki, Tamba no koyuki", is "powder-snow", used because the snow falls like rice powder after pounding and husking. The second line, which should be *tamare koyuki*, has been corrupted to *Tamba no koyuki*. One authority has claimed that the line after that should be, "On fences and the crotches of trees." I wonder if this expression dates back to antiquity. The Emperor Toba, as a boy, used *koyuki* to describe falling snow, as we know, from the diary of Sanuki no Suke.' Keene, *Tsurezuregusa*, p. 156.

15. Nagako was in fact the younger sister, not the daughter, of Emperor Horikawa's nurse, but this statement does suggest that she was the right age to be described as an *onmenotogo*.

16. Emperor Toba, then Crown Prince, had resided at the Kokiden from 25-12-1105 to 7-2-1106 and from 27-6-1106 to 17-9-1106.

17. During the period of state mourning the bamboo-blinds (*misu*) of the Seiryōden were replaced by blinds made from rushes, with borders of slate-grey material. All the other drapes were also of slate-grey, while the wooden borders of the screens were of whitewood. The curtain-dais was removed from both the Daytime Chamber and Imperial Bedchamber, and straw mats covered the floor. The backless chair (*daishōji*) used for dressing the Emperor's hair was also removed from the Imperial Washing Room.

18. By Nagako's account, these events took place on the third day of the first month, but according to the *Chūyūki* the Regent Tadazane did not attend court on the third day because of a taboo.

19. A divided silk skirt, or loose trousers of laced (or threaded) silk (*sashinuki*) was part of the ordinary court costume.

20. Horikawa's Empress, Atsuko, retired from the world on 21-9-1107, and initiated Buddhist memorial services for the late Emperor at the Horikawa Palace. A section of the *Lotus Sutra* was copied each day, and the *Chūyūki* records that on 19-1-1108, there was a dedication of a Buddhist sutra by the Empress after the memorial service.

21. This section is rather obscure, and Tamai has not attempted to give any notes. I have followed Ishii's interpretation. The connection between this section and the rest of the work is unclear.

22. The *shushōe* (*sujōe*) was a Buddhist ceremony, starting on the first day of the first month and lasting from three to seven days, during which prayers were offered for the peace of the realm.

23. Taifu no suke may have been the daughter of Minamoto no Akinaka, who, with her two sisters, was a well-known poetess. Naishi's identity is not known.

24. The unknown person whom Nagako and her friends met at the temple seems

to be the same person whose anniversary service Nagako attended in the second month of 1108.

25. *Inishie ni | Iro mo kawarazu | Sakinikeri | Hana koso mono wa | Omowazarikere.* A poem by Hata no Kanekata very similar to this is included in the Miscellaneous section of the *Kinyōshū*, prefaced with the words—'Written on seeing the flowering blossoms in the spring of the year following the death of Emperor Go-Sanjō.' (*Kozo mishi ni | Iro mo kawarazu | Sakinikeri | Hana koso mono wa | Omowazarikere.*)

True indeed<br>
That flowers have no feelings!<br>
For here they are blooming<br>
With colours bright as last year.

As the *Kinyōshū* was not completed until 1127, it is likely that Nagako took her version of the poem from the now lost *Kanekata Shū* referred to in the *Minamoto no Michinari Shū*. See *GR*, vol. IX, p. 701, and Imai, *Nikki kenkyū*, p. 355.

The Emperor is mistakenly referred to as Emperor Sanjō, but I have followed common practice in correcting this to Go-Sanjō.

26. Seiryōden here refers to the part of the Horikawa Palace used as the imperial residence. The members of the Emperor's Private Office (*kurōdodokoro*) seem to have had their quarters (*kurōdomachi*) in the stables to the south-west of the Palace, while the various military guards were housed in an outhouse to the south of the eastern central gate.

The Emperor's Private Office contained approximately twenty people—two Chief Chamberlains, three third-rank Chamberlains, four of sixth rank, four to six *hikurōdo*, and about eight *kaeritenjō*.

The *Chūyūki* has the following entry for 23-9-1107: 'Next, the appointed evening service commenced. From today, Buddhist services are to be held at set times morning and evening until the end of the mourning period. This is the order of the Empress. The six priests appointed to this duty are to be housed in the quarters of the Emperor's Private Office.'

27. This poem (*Kage dani mo | Tomarazarikeru | Kumo no ue wo | Tama no utena to | Tare ka iiken*) occurs in the *Iwakage* chapter of *Eiga Monogatari*, prefaced by the words—'Composed by Jōtōmon'in on seeing the place where the late Emperor had dwelled, bright in the dazzling radiance of the moonlight.' It was presumably so well known that Nagako felt justified in omitting both the names of the deceased Emperor Ichijō (968–1011), and of his consort, Jōtōmon'in or Akiko.

Since the poem was inspired by the moonlight, it employs several words or phrases associated with the moon, e.g. *kage* (shadow), *kumo no ue* (above the clouds—a phrase often used of themselves by members of Heian society), *tama no utena*—jewelled tower—probably borrowed from Chinese literature, c.f. Morris, Ivan (trans.), *The Pillow Book of Sei Shōnagon* (N.Y., 1967), vol. II, p. 67.

28. The Thirty Readings (*Sanjikkō*) consisted of the reading of the twenty-eight chapters of the *Hokekyō*, together with the prologue, *Muryōgikyō*, and epilogue, *Fugenkankyō*. The reading was conducted either once a day for thirty days, or morning and evening for fifteen days.

    The *Chūyūki* (26–2–1108) records, 'Towards evening I visited the Empress. For the past 21 days she has had one chapter of the sutra read each day.'

29. The ceremony of changing clothes was held twice yearly. On the first day of the tenth month everyone changed into winter clothes, and on the first day of the fourth month everyone changed into summer clothes. The curtains and other drapes were changed to a lighter material in summer.

30. A ceremony (*kambutsue, buttane*) was held on the eighth day of the fourth month to celebrate the birth of the historical Buddha Sakyamuni. Coloured water was sprinkled over an image of Buddha.

    All the lords and ladies-in-waiting would bring forth offerings for the Buddhist monks taking part in the ceremony. These would be offered in front of the Buddha before the ceremony began. Initially money was offered, but later paper was offered. The court ladies, however, went to great pains to present beautifully designed and decorated offerings.

    *Gōke shidai* records that at this ceremony the bamboo blinds in the Daytime Chamber were lowered, and the throne removed. Two stands for the Buddha-image were placed in the fourth bay of the eastern ante-room, and two black-lacquered tables placed on either side of these. In the first and second bays of the outer ante-room, hard against the eastern edge, *tatami* were spread out as seating for the Princes and Nobles.

31. Formal dress, for men, on such a ceremonial occasion, included a short-sleeved under-robe (*shitagasane*) with a train (*shiri*).

    The outer ante-room (*hirobisashi*) is an area which serves in fact as an ante-room to the ante-room (*hisashi*). Both are covered areas adjacent to the main room (*moya*) and bordered on the outer edge by the open verandah (*sunoko*). There were four ante-rooms—the northern, southern, eastern and western—according to the direction in which each lay off the main room.

32. This sentence is obscure. The phrase I have translated as 'the mountain-shaped cones' (*yama no zasu*) is probably a reference to the *yamagata*—cone-shaped objects placed on either side of the Buddha-platform.

    The phrase translated as 'the five coloured waters' (*koshiki no wataru*) is probably a reference to the water used for sprinkling on the statue. There were five different colours—bluish-green, red, white, yellow and black.

33. These were Horikawa's uncles, the Minamoto brothers Masatoshi and Kunizane.

34. The fifth day of the fifth month was the Iris Festival. On the evening of the

fourth day it was the duty of members of the Office of Grounds (*tonomoryō*) to decorate the Palace roofs with irises.

Mizu Field lay at the confluence of three rivers outside Kyoto, and its name became famous as a pillow word (*makura kotoba*). It is now contained in Fushimi Ward of modern Kyoto.

35. The *saishōkō* was the annual discourse upon the *Konkōmyō saishōō kyō* or *Sutra of the Golden Light* held in the Imperial Palace over a five day period in the fifth month, by the priests of the Tōdaiji, Kōfukuji, Enryakuji and Onjōji. The purpose of the ceremony was to pray for peace for the realm.

*Denreki* (22–5–1109) records that the *saishōkō* was held on that date for the first time during the reign of Emperor Toba.

36. The location of this spot (*Horikawa izumi*) is not known. It could not have been the Horikawa Water Palace (*izumidono*), as the Horikawa Palace did not boast such a building.

37. Fan-lottery (*ōgibiki*) seems to have been a game of chance, in which fans were drawn as lots. Poems may have been composed about the painting decorating each fan.

38. An interesting use of the feudal term 'houseman' (*ie no ko*), used of a vassal connected by blood ties to his lord.

39. The 49th day ceremony is recorded in the *Chūyūki* as having been held on 7–9–1107, with 107 priests officiating. There is no account of this ceremony in Nagako's work as it now stands.

40. *Chūyūki* (7–9–1107) records that six or seven ladies-in-waiting who had served the Emperor for a long time stayed on at the Horikawa Palace at the request of the Empress. Only one, Suō no naishi, is mentioned by name, but the others are probably the same as those listed on 24–7–1107 as being given mourning robes, i.e. Izumo, Shin Shōnagon, Mutsu, Yamato, Emon and Bingo.

41. During a period of mourning the ribbons (*ei*) which hung down at the back of the ceremonial cap (*kōburi*) were looped up.

42. The meaning of part of this sentence is obscure.

43. Cords (*motoyui*) made of silk, hemp or paper were used for tying up the hair. A mottled effect (*murago*) could be achieved by uneven dying. Hairpins (*saishi*) were also used to keep the hair in place.

44. See Section One, note 6.

45. This poem (*Mina hito wa / Hana no tamoto ni / Narinunari / Koke no koromo yo / Kawaki dani seyo*) is a misquote of the following poem, which is found in the Grief section of the *Kokinshū* (poem no. 847): *Mina hito wa / Hana no koromo ni / Narinunari / Koke no tamoto yo / Kawaki dani seyo*. Its author, Bishop Henjo, was in lay life Yoshimine no Munesada and a famous poet. He was very close to Emperor Nimmyō (833–850), who was also known, after his burial mound at Fukakusa in the Kii district of Yamashiro province, as Fukakusa no Mikado.

46. It was customary when an Emperor changed residence for fire and water to be carried from the old residence to the new. *Denreki* (21–8–1108) records that the procession to the Imperial Palace was led by four girl attendants. One on the right carried the fire, one on the left carried the water, and the other two led oxen. It seems that such girls were supplied from the household of an Imperial Nurse or someone in close attendance on the Emperor.

47. The *mizura* or *onbinzura* style was one worn by young boys. The hair was parted down the centre and looped into a bunch over each ear.

48. *Denreki* puts the time at about 8 p.m.

49. The Central Gate (*Naka no mikado*) refers to the Taiken Mon, the main eastern gate of the Greater Imperial Palace.

50. The Kōryūji was Emperor Horikawa's burial place. It was located to the north-west of Kyoto in Igasa village, near the present Hirano shrine. Horikawa was cremated in a field to the south-west of the Kōryūji, and it was intended that his remains be taken to the tumulus of Emperor Enyū at the Ninnaji. However, because this lay in a forbidden direction, the Emperor's remains were for some time deposited in the priests' quarters at the Kōryūji before a provisional tumulus was built. It was only intended that the Emperor's remains rest at the Kōryūji for three years, but it was not until the 22nd day of the third month, 1113, that Horikawa's remains were moved to the Ninnaji.

51. *Denreki* records that the move was made on the 25th day of the 12th month, 1106.

52. Much of this passage is obscure. The storehouse (*kurabeya*) was a building near the Seiryōden, which may have served as living quarters for some of the ladies-in-waiting.

53. The remainder of the sentence is obscure.

54. The Imperial Guards (*takiguchi*) were a body of twenty men attached to the Emperor's Private Office (*kurōdodokoro*) and responsible for guarding the Palace. Every night at 9 p.m. there was a roll-call (*nadaimen*) of the Senior Courtiers on duty at the Palace, followed by a muster (*monjaku*) of the Imperial Guards of the Emperor's Private Office. A Chamberlain of the sixth rank would call, 'Who is present?' and each member of the Guard would twang his bow-string and announce his name. This ritual was observed at various places, starting with the northern guard-house (*kita no jin*) and including the alleyway beside the Imperial Bathing Room (*miyudono*), and the eastern doorway of the Senior Courtiers' Chamber (*tenjō no ma*). The alleyway beside the Imperial Bathing Room, which was in the north-west corner of the Seiryōden, probably refers to the bridle-path (*medō*) between the Bathing Room and the eastern ante-room of the Kōryōden.

55. The text of these two sentences has been corrupted. I have followed the suggestions of Ishii and Kakimoto Susumu.

The Inner Palace Guards of the Left would call the hours of the night from

9 p.m. to 12.30 a.m., while the Inner Palace Guards of the Right would call the hours from 1 a.m. to 4.30 a.m. The term *fushō* was used of lower-ranking members of the Palace Guards and Imperial Police. At the last quarter of every watch (i.e. every two hours), members of the Time Office (*tokizukasa*) would go to the courtyard outside the Seiryōden, and inscribe the time on a board (*toki no fuda*). One of the Guards would then attach the board to a post (*toki no kui*).

56. The language here indicates that this is a reference to a poem, or perhaps the draft of a poem.

57. The expression 'the sleeve that once entwined my beloved' (*katashiki no sode*) was often used in love poems, while the fishing allusion was a fairly common poetic conceit.

58. The Black Door (*kurodo*) was the door leading to the gallery at the north of the Seiryōden, which led to the Kokiden, the residence of the Empress. The name was also applied to the gallery itself.

59. The Jijūden was a palace to the east of the Seiryōden, from which it was separated by a courtyard. It was at one time the residence of the Emperor, but was later used for banquets, contests, etc.

The Table Room (*daihandokoro*) was a large room on the western side of the Seiryōden, adjoining the Imperial Dining Room (*asagarei no ma*). It was used mainly by ladies-in-waiting on duty.

The screen with the scene of Lake Kommei (*kommeichi no misōji*) was a single-leafed sliding screen on stands situated in the eastern outer ante-room of the Seiryōden, and adjacent to the partition between the chapel (*futama*) and the room used by the Empress (*kokiden no ue no mitsubone*). On the southern side of the screen was a painting of Lake Kommei, an artificial lake created by a Chinese emperor to the south-west of the city of Ch'ang-an, for the purpose of practising naval manoeuvres.

60. The eastern side of the Black Door Gallery was lined with small hinged half-shutters (*kohajitomi*), made of lattice-work, which could be raised to let in more light. Outside the shutters lay a garden, through which ran a small stream (*mikawamizu*), which circuited the courtyard on the eastern side of the Seiryōden.

61. This poem is included in the Grief section of the *Kokinshū* (poem no. 853). Nothing is known about its author, Miharu no Arisuke, except that he came from Kōchi, held sixth rank, and was a Captain of the Outer Palace Guards of the Left.

62. The bush-clover or *Lespedeza bicolor* is known in Japan as *hagi*. It produces a reddish-purple flower.

63. The Bush-clover Door (*hagi no to*) was a room adjoining the Black Door, and was situated between the room used by the Empress from the Kokiden, and the room used by the Empress from the Fujitsubo (*Fujitsubo no ue no mitsubone*).

The name was derived from a sliding-screen decorated with paintings of bush-clover flowers. It is actually doubtful if the garden could be seen from this room.

The Sogyōden (or Shōkyōden) was a palace to the north of the Jijūden, used for the purpose of banquets and entertainments. The identity of the person of whom Nagako is reminded by the sight of this building is not known.

64. The Chrysanthemum Festival (*chōyō, kikku no sekku*) was one of the Five Palace Festivals (*gosekku*). It was held on the 9th day of the 9th month. The Emperor and court would inspect the chrysanthemums in the Palace grounds, after which a banquet was held, at which poems were composed, and wine in which chrysanthemums had been steeped was drunk.

65. The screen dividing the Imperial Dining Room from the Table Room was in *yamato-e* style, while the screen dividing the Dining Room from the Imperial Washing Room had a cat painted on one side, and birds and bamboo on the other.

66. The Great Festival of Thanksgiving (*daijōe, daijōsai*) was a Shinto ceremony which took place once in the reign of each Emperor, shortly after the accession. It corresponded to the annual Festival of the First Fruits (*niiname-sai*). The new Emperor worshipped the ancestral deities of heaven and earth in a solemn, traditional feast of new grain.

The Great Purification (*gokei, ōharae*) generally refers to a national ceremony held twice yearly to rid the whole nation of defilement and offences to the deities. Here it refers to the ritual purification of the Emperor necessary for him to take part in the Great Festival of Thanksgiving. On this occasion the ceremony of ritual ablution was performed on the banks of the Kamo River in the vicinity of Reizei Road.

Some texts give the date as the eleventh day, but this could well have been a copyist's error.

67. Fujiwara no Nagazane had succeeded Fujiwara no Mototake, the previously-mentioned Governor of Harima, in the seventh month of 1108. Some texts give the name as Narizane.

68. This was Fujiwara no Akitaka, who was dressed in the over-robe (*ue no kinu*) worn on ceremonial court occasions. It was scarlet in accordance with his fifth-rank position.

69. The Chamberlain was Fujiwara no Tametaka, who had been a Chamberlain during Horikawa's reign, but who actually no longer held the office. *Denreki* (21–10–1108) records, 'Tametaka reported that the carriage bearing the Acting Imperial Lady was in Ōmiya Avenue.'

On the procession to the spot where the Great Purification was held, the Emperor would be accompanied by a girl representing an Imperial Lady, and known as a *nyōgodai*. When the Emperor was young, the daughter of a Great

Minister or Major Counsellor was chosen. On this occasion the girl was the 14-year old daughter of the Regent.

This sentence is slightly obscure.

70. The Empress Mother (*kisai no miya*) was Emperor Shirakawa's daughter, Princess Yoshiko, who was Emperor Toba's foster-mother, and had been raised to the position on his accession. She was to travel in the same carriage as Toba, because of his youth.

71. The Special Festivals (*rinji no matsuri*) were Shinto festivals held annually at the Kamo Shrines in the eleventh month, and the Iwashimizu Hachiman Shrine in the third month. They were known as 'special' to distinguish them from the Kamo Festival held in the fourth month. In 1108, the Special Festival was postponed to the twelfth month, as the eleventh month was taken up with the Great Festival of Thanksgiving.

The *Gosechi* celebrations were court dances performed in the eleventh month by young girls of good family, in association with the Festival of the First Fruits (*niiname-sai*). Normally the celebrations lasted for four days in the middle of the month, and were as follows:

| | |
|---|---|
| Day of the Ox: | Dais Rehearsal (*chōdai no kokoromi*)—a formal dress-rehearsal of the Gosechi dances in the Jōneiden in the presence of the Emperor, who was seated on his curtain-dais (*chōdai*). |
| Day of the Tiger: | Senior Courtiers' Banquet (*tenjō no enzui*) with poetry and dancing, followed by dances in the Seiryōden in the presence of the Emperor and Court (*omae no kokoromi*). |
| Day of the Hare: | Attendants' Dance (*warawamai*)—the girl assistants (*warawa*) who dressed the dancers' hair and helped with their costumes, danced in the Seiryōden before the Emperor. |
| | Tasting of the First Fruits (*niiname-sai*)—the Emperor made offerings of the first-fruits of the grain harvest, and partook thereof himself. |
| Day of the Dragon: | The Gosechi Dances were performed as part of the *toyo no akari no sechie*, a night of celebrations, during which the newly-harvested rice was consumed at a banquet, which was followed by the dances, and the award of gift-robes and ranks. |

In the year of a Great Festival of Thanksgiving (*daijōsai*), however, the celebrations lasted for six days, with the following additions:

| | |
|---|---|
| Day of the Hare: | Attendants' Dance, Great Festival of Thanksgiving. |
| Day of the Dragon: | *Yuki no sechie*—the offering of the new season's rice from one of the eastern provinces. |

Day of the Serpent:    *Suki no sechie*—the offering of the new season's rice from one of the western provinces.

*Seishodō no mikagura*—a *kagura* performance consisting of Shinto songs and dances to a musical accompaniment, held in the Seishodō, a palace within the Burakuin palace complex, which was used specifically for *kagura* performances.

Day of the Horse:    Gosechi Dances.

Normally there would be four girl dancers, two from High Court Noble families, and two from Senior Courtier and provincial governor families. In the year of a Great New Food Festival there would be five dancers, the one extra girl coming from a High Court Noble family.

72. After the banquet, which was held on the night of the Day of the Tiger, those present would wander about the palace in varying degrees of intoxication. They would relax, bare-shouldered, with one sleeve hanging down.

73. Nagako was probably in the *kokiden no ue no mitsubone*.

74. *Chūyūki* (13–11–1106) records that the Dais Rehearsal went on till about 10 p.m., and that there was a light sprinkling of snow.

It was customary for participants in Shinto ceremonies to wear head-decorations made of white and blue braid looped in a clover shape, to represent a lycopodium plant. These were known as *hikage no kazura*, and the Gosechi dancers attached four to either end of their ornamental hair-pins.

75. A temporary arched bridge was constructed to connect the Emperor's residential palace, the Seiryōden, with the Shōkyōden to the north-east. The Shōkyōden, which was used for banquets and entertainments, connected to the Jōneiden, where the girl dancers were housed and where the Dais Rehearsal was held.

76. The phrase 'to name one as a plum tree' (*izure wo ume to waki*) is a reference to a poem by Ki no Tomonori in the Winter section of the *Kokinshū* (poem no. 337): *Yuki fureba | Kigoto ni hana zo | Sakinikeru | Izure wo ume to | Wakite oramashi.*

> The trees are blossom-decked
> With freshly-fallen snow,
> And one would have to break a spray
> To name one as a plum tree.

77. The garden between the Seiryōden and the Jijūden to the east contained two thickets of bamboo. The southernmost thicket, closest to the Seiryōden, was of long-jointed bamboo (*kawatake*), while the northernmost one, closest to the Jijūden, was a species of black bamboo (*kuretake*). Near this latter thicket was a fire-hut (*hitakiya*), a small, roofless hut of the sort used for the bonfires that illuminated the Palace gardens. Around the northern edge of the garden, running from the guard-house of the Imperial Guards to the north-east corner

of the Seiryōden, was a fence made of board or bamboo with interstices (*suigai*).

78. A set of autumn-coloured robes (*momiji-gasane*) consisted of eight unlined robes—three yellow (*kiiro*), one each of light and dark gold (*yamabuki*), one each of light and dark crimson (*kurenai*), and one dark red (*suō*).

79. This passage is rather obscure. The syllables *uchiheku* in the text may be a corruption of *uchitsukuri*, meaning an artisan; while *yari* may be an abbreviation of *yariganna*, a type of carpenter's plane.

80. Most of this section concerns the Chrysanthemum Festival (*kiku no sekku*, *chōyō*) which customarily took place on the ninth day of the ninth month. One of the most memorable sights of the festival was the display of the robes of the ladies-in-waiting from beneath curtains of state decorated with artificial chrysanthemums. The ladies wore sets of robes in the *momijigasane* combination, or the *kikugasane* combination, which was a set of eight unlined robes— the upper five being in shades of dark red (*suō*), becoming progressively lighter towards the inside, and the lower three being white. The sleeves of each robe were shorter than the one beneath it, so the careful blending of colours was seen to its best advantage in the sleeve-openings (*sodeguchi*).

The Narrow Corridor (*Hosodono*) was the western ante-room of the Kokiden Palace, where the Empress Mother, Princess Yoshiko, resided.

81. This was probably the *kokiden no ue no mitsubone*.

82. A set of twelve unlined robes in shades of yellowish green (*aoiro*) and dark red (*suō*) was known as *ryūtan* (*rindō*) *gasane*. Nagako's Chinese jacket (*karaginu*) was of purple-red (*akairo*).

83. The *kagura* performance in the Seishodō was a traditional part of the celebrations held in conjunction with the Great Festival of Thanksgiving. Actually, however, at Toba's accession the Great Festival of Thanksgiving took place in the Daigokuden, and the *kagura* performance in the Koadono (Shōanden, Oyasumidokoro) to the north of the Daigokuden. The *kagura* is probably here spoken of as the *Seishodō no mikagura* through force of habit.

84. Izumi was probably the name of one of Nagako's attendants. The Emperor makes a play on the words *izumi*, meaning spring, and *ike*, meaning pool.

85. This was probably the morning of the 21st, and Nagako supposes that the Senior Courtiers are still feeling the effects of the banquets and dances the previous evening.

86. Lady Yamato is probably the same court lady given mourning robes on Horikawa's death (see *Chūyūki* 24-7-1107).

87. According to legend, a group of heavenly maidens appeared to Emperor Temmu while he was playing the cithern at the Yoshino Palace, and danced to his music, shaking their feathered sleeves five times.

88. Nagako's reply is rather obscure. It may refer to an ancient belief that an

Emperor did not die, but merely slept later than usual, to appear in his palanquin when the sun was high in the sky.

89. Emperor Toba went to the Daigokuden on the night of the 21st, and after the Great Festival of Thanksgiving moved into the Koadono. He returned to the Seiryōden on the night of the 24th.

90. It is not clear why everyone should be familiar with the Great Festival of Thanksgiving, since it occurred only once in each reign. Perhaps Nagako was writing with a certain group of readers in mind, and knew they had all been present at the ceremony themselves.

91. The *kagura* took place on the night of the 23rd day. Every year a propitious day was selected in the twelfth month for a *kagura* performance in the garden of the Ummeiden (the present Kashikodokoro), a building in the Greater Imperial Palace where the Sacred Mirror was guarded by members of the Palace Attendants' Office (*naishi no tsukasa*). The Ummeiden was therefore also known as the Palace Attendants' Office (*naishidokoro*).

92. A special unlined over-robe (*omigoromo*) was worn by participants in Shinto ceremonies. The robe was white with a blue pattern, and a pair of red ribbons (*himo*) was draped over the right shoulder. White and blue braids (*hikage no kazura*) were attached to the ceremonial caps. The participants in the *kagura* performance wore artificial flowers (*kazashi no hana*) on their ceremonial caps, similar to those worn by participants in the Special Festival. Imperial envoys (*tsukai*) wore wistaria, while the dancers and musicians wore cherry-blossom or yellow roses. *Chūyūki* (23-11-1108) records that the Regent wore wistaria, Counsellors wore plum-blossom, and Imperial Advisers wore yellow roses (*yamabuki*). *Gōke shidai* records that Princes wore plum-blossom, the Regent wistaria, Counsellors cherry-blossom, and Imperial Advisers yellow roses.

93. *Kagura* songs consist of two parts—*motouta* and *sueuta*, which I have translated as versicle and response respectively—terms which seem appropriate in view of the semi-religious nature of the *kagura*. The singers are divided accordingly into two groups, each with its own chorus-leader who beat the time with wooden clappers (*shakubyōshi, sakuhōshi*). *Chūyūki* (23-11-1108) records that Fujiwara no Munemichi was the chorus-leader for the versicles (*motobyōshi*), while Fujiwara no Munetada (the author of *Chūyūki*) was the chorus-leader for the responses (*suebyōshi*). The role of the Regent, Fujiwara no Tadazane, is not quite clear, but it seems that he acted as overall conductor.

94. Only Ministers of the Left, Right and Centre were permitted to wear wistaria blossom, and the Regent, who combined the position of Minister of the Right, was the only one present holding such a position.

95. The Inspector Middle Counsellor was Fujiwara no Munemichi. The title *Azechi* was originally given to provincial inspectors, but later the post became a sinecure awarded to officials with the position of Middle Counsellor or above. The text in this passage has been slightly corrupted, and it seems that the

syllables *fue so* have been omitted. As the account goes on to say, 'the flute and flageolet were played by the same people as before', I have corrected this mistake according to the *Chūyūki* account.

The flute (*fue*) referred to is the *kagura-bue* or *Yamato-bue*, a six-holed flute made of bamboo and claimed as an original Japanese creation, though modified under Chinese influence in the Nara and Heian periods. The cithern (*wagon*, *Yamato-goto*, *koto*) is a six-stringed instrument, tuned by placing a bridge, originally the forked branch of a tree, under each string. It also is claimed as a Japanese creation. The flageolet (*hichiriki*) is a nine-holed double-reed instrument. These three instruments constitute the basic *kagura* trio, the last two being the melodic instruments, and the cithern providing both melody and harmony.

96. This song is as follows:

| | |
|---|---|
| Versicle: | Senzai senzai, |
| | Senzai ya senzai ya, |
| | Chitose no senzai ya. |
| Response: | Manzai manzai, |
| | Manzai ya manzai ya, |
| | Yorozuyo no manzai ya. |
| Versicle: | Nao senzai. |
| Response: | Nao manzai. |
| Versicle: | Senzai senzai senzai ya, |
| | Chitose no senzai ya. |
| Response: | Manzai manzai manzai ya, |
| | Yorozuyo no manzai ya. |

The *kagura* is said to have originated in the attempts of the gods to lure the Sun Goddess, Amaterasu, from the rock-cave in which she was sulking, by performing songs and dances.

97. Nagai beach (*Nagai no ura*) is a pillow word. The beach may have been situated in the present Nagai quarter of the Sumiyoshi district of Osaka city, or may have been an ocean beach at the port of Itozaki in the district of Mitsugi in Bingo province. A reference is probably intended also to *Kokinshū* poem no. 1085: *Kimi ga yo wa | Kagiri mo araji | Nagahama no | Masago no kazu wa | Yomitsukusu to mo.*

> Though the grains of sand
> On Nagahama Beach be counted,
> May the years of your life
> Remain forever countless.

98. The Mimosuso River is a name found often in congratulatory poems. It is another name for the Isuzu River, which flows in front of the Inner Shrine (*Naikū*) of the Great Shrines at Ise. The phrase *Mimosusogawa no nagare* is often used to refer to the imperial descendants of Amaterasu.

The phrase 'the mountainous years of his reign' (*kurai no yama no toshi*) is also often found in congratulatory poems.

99. The reference to the camellia (*shiratama tsubaki yachiyo ni chiyo wo souru*) is a reference to a poem by Fujiwara no Sukenari in the Felicitations section of the *Goshūishū* (poem no. 453): *Kimi ga yo wa | Shiratama tsubaki | Yachiyo tomo | Nani ni kazoemu | Kagiri nakareba.*

> The jewel-white camellia
> Lives eight thousand years,
> But with what can I compare
> The years of my lord's life—
> For they are countless.

The phrase 'the waves of the seas of the four quarters' (*yomo no umi no nami*) is again found frequently in congratulatory poems.

1. The main *kagura* performance was followed by impromptu performances (*miasobi*). In the group performance described here, the lute (*biwa*), a pear-shaped instrument with four strings and four frets and played with a small plectrum (*bachi*), is played by Minamoto no Mototsuna; while the reed pipes (*shō*), an exotic type of pipe organ consisting of seventeen reed pipes placed in a cup-shaped wind chest, and capable of producing beautiful chords, was played by Minamoto no Masasada.

This account contains two errors, (a) that Munetada was the chorus leader as before (*moto no gotoku Munetada no Chūnagon*)—Munetada was not mentioned in the earlier account, and himself records in the *Chūyūki* that Munemichi was the chorus leader, (b) Masasada's name is written as Masatada.

2. The tune 'Ten Thousand Years' (*Manzairaku*) was based on the mode E and supposed to represent the call of a phoenix or parrot. On festive occasions it would be accompanied by a dance performed by six people.

*Ana tōtō* and *Ise no umi* are *saibara*, or songs which originated in folk songs sung by peasants, especially while leading their horses, but to which variations were added with the introduction of Chinese music, and which by the Heian period were included in the ceremonial court music (*gagaku*) repertoire.

*Ana tōtō* is in the *ryo* mode, and is as follows:

> Ana tōtō, kyō no tōtosa ya, inishie mo, hare.
> Inishie mo, kaku ya arikemu ya, kyō no tōtosa.
> Aware, sokoyoshi ya, kyō no tōtosa.

> How august! Ah! even in the past
> Was there aught to rival today's augustness?
> Could there have been anything like
> Today's augustness, even in the past?
> Ah! how magnificent is today's augustness.

*Ise no umi* is in the *ritsu* mode, and is as follows:

Ise no umi no
Kiyoki nagisa ni
Shiogai ni
Nanoriso ya tsumamu
Kai ya hirowamu
Tama ya hirowamu ya.

On the azure strand
Of the Ise sea
When the tide is low,
Let us gather seaweed,
Let us collect seashells,
Let us collect gemstones.

3. Munetada records in the *Chūyūki* that he sang in the chorus during these songs.

4. Those who took part in the performance were rewarded by the Emperor with gift-robes. *Chūyūki* records that Tadazane received a white formal Court robe (*ōuchigi*), an under-robe (*shitagasane*), a short-sleeved jacket (*hampi*) and a trouser-skirt (*hakama*).

   Mt Mikasa is in Nara city, and rises behind the Kasuga Shrine, where the Fujiwara family honoured their ancestral gods.

5. Tadazane was aged 31 at the time.

   The Wheel-Rolling King or *Tenrin shōō* (*Cakravartin*, *Cakravarti-rāja*) was a king who ruled the world by rolling a wheel given to him by heaven at his enthronement. There were four types of wheel—the Gold-Wheel-Rolling King ruled the four continents; the Silver-Wheel-Rolling King, the eastern, western and southern continents; the Copper-Wheel-Rolling King, the eastern and southern continents; and the Iron-Wheel-Rolling King, the southern continent.

6. Tadazane's son, Tadamichi, was aged 13 at the time, and was a Middle Captain of the Inner Palace Guards of the Right.

7. The imagery in this sentence is of the type often used in congratulatory poems.

8. This was the 24th day of the 11th month, the day after the *kagura* performance.

9. The meaning of these two poems (*Mezurashiki | Toyo no akari no | Hikage ni mo | Narenishi kumo no | Ue zo koishiki*) and (*Omoiyaru | Toyo no akari no | Kuma naki ni | Yoso naru hito no | Sode zo sobotsuru*) is enhanced by the use of *engo* (words with associated meanings) e.g. *akari* in the phrase *toyo no akari* (an abbreviation for the *toyo no akari no sechie* or Festival of the First Fruits) is associated with *hikage*, *hikage* with *kumo*, and *akari* with *kumanashi*.

10. These two lines are necessary to translate Nagako's phrase *wakare ya itodo*, which is virtually meaningless in itself, but which is taken from a poem sent by Ki no Tsurayuki to Fujiwara no Kanesuke at the end of the year in which Kanesuke's wife had died. The poem is contained in the Grief sections of both *Gosenshū* and *Shūishū*: *Kouru ma ni | Toshi no kurenaba | Naki hito no | Wakare ya itodo | Tōku narinamu.*

Should the New Year catch you
Still grieving for your beloved,
That last parting would slip
Yet deeper into the past.

The phrase is actually incorrectly given as *wakare ya isa* in all extant texts, but as the phrase is later given correctly, the discrepancy is probably a copyist's error.

11. This poem by the Master of the Buddhist Law, Nōin, is included in the Grief section of the *Goshūishū*.

12. This poem (*Nagekitsutsu / Toshi no kurenaba / Naki hito no / Wakare ya itodo / Tōku narinamu*) is a variation on the poem by Ki no Tsurayuki referred to in Section 51. Parts of the preceding section are slightly obscure. For instance, the words 'in the case of the discussions on the Buddhist sutras' (*kayō no hōmon*) would normally refer to a lecture or sermon on Buddhism which had just been described, but the only such descriptions occur in sections 35 and 42. I have followed Ishii in interpreting the phrase *nyōbōshu* as 'mistress' rather than 'all the ladies-in-waiting'.

13. It is not clear in which year this visit to the Kōryūji was made.

14. This poem, in slightly altered form, is included in the Third Miscellaneous section of the *Shinchokusenshū*. It is attributed to Horikawa in Sanuki no Suke, and follows three poems by Minamoto no Kunizane, on the subject of Horikawa's burial place at the Kōryūji, to which are given the year period Juei (1182–1183). As such a date is impossible, it seems that the characters for Juei were written in error for the very similar characters for Kajō (1106–1107).

15. This sentence actually reads 'Kore wo aru hito ii-okosetari' or 'A certain person sent me this poem'. This could refer to either the preceding or the following poem, but I have taken it to refer to the preceding poem, and have added the word 'last' to make it clear that this was a reply to the two poems which Nagako composed on the subject of the pampas grasses.

16. This exchange of poems would seem more suitably placed at the end of the work, as it obviously refers to a completed work. Nagako's poem (*Omoiyare / Nagusamu ya tote / Kaki-okishi / Koto no ha sae zo / Mireba kanashiki*) reiterates the phrase *nagusamu ya* which occurs in the closing lines of section 1.

17. I have followed Ishii in interpreting *kono mikado* as 'these three conditions' rather than 'this emperor', the three conditions given being that the person should remember Emperor Horikawa affectionately, should be well-disposed towards Nagako herself, and should be someone with friends and influence. The actual identity of Lady Hitachi is unknown, though it has been suggested (a) that she may be the same person referred to as Bingo in the *Chūyūki* 24-7-1107 record of the six ladies-in-waiting given mourning clothes to wear for Emperor Horikawa, (b) that she was Daini no sammi Ieko, who was also known as Hitachi no suke.

# BIBLIOGRAPHY

WORKS RELATING SPECIFICALLY TO *Sanuki no Suke Nikki*

Fujida Kazu. '*Sanuki no Suke Nikki* dembon kō', *Heian bungaku kenkyū*, vol. XVI (Dec. 1954).

Imai Gen'e. '*Sanuki no Suke Nikki*', *Kokubungaku kaishaku to kanshō*, vol. XXVI, no. 2 (Feb. 1961).

Imakōji Kakuzui and Mitani Sachiko. *Kōhon Sanuki no Suke Nikki*, Tokyo: Hatsune Shobō, 1967.

———. *Kōchū Sanuki no Suke Nikki*, Tokyo: Ryūkan Shoin, 1976.

Inaga Keiji. '*Sanuki no Suke Nikki* no shi to sei—sukebara no mikotachi', *Kokubungaku*, vol. X, no. 14 (Dec. 1965).

Ishii Fumio. *Sanuki no Suke Nikki*, in *Nihon koten bungaku zenshū*, vol. XVIII, Tokyo: Shogakukan, 1971.

Ishino Keiko. '*Sanuki no Suke Nikki*', *Kokubungaku*, vol. X, no. 4 (Mar. 1965).

Kakimoto Tsutomu. 'Kyūtei josei no kokoro—shi—*Sanuki no Suke Nikki* no baai', *Kokubungaku kaishaku to kanshō*, vol. XXXI (Mar. 1966).

———. '*Sanuki no Suke Nikki* no hombun seiri', *Osaka kyōiku daigaku kiyō*, vol. XVI, no. 1 (1967).

———. '*Sanuki no Suke Nikki* oboegaki—itsu, hombun ni tsuite', *Kaishaku*, vol. XI, no. 1 (Jan. 1965).

Kaneko Eiji. '*Kiyokinagisa no shū* to *Sanuki no Suke Nikki*', *Kokugo to kokubungaku*, vol. XIV (Nov. 1937).

Katagiri Yō'ichi. 'Kōhon *Sanuki no Suke Nikki*', in *Matsukage kokubun shiryō sōkan*, vol. I, Tokyo: Matsukage Joshi Gakuin Daigaku, 1966.

Mabuchi Kazuo. 'Asahi koten zensho *Sanuki no Suke Nikki* ni furete', *Heian bungaku kenkyū*, vol. XV (June 1954)

———. 'Ozaki Satoakira shi hen *Sanuki no Suke Nikki*', *Heian bungaku kenkyū*, vol. XXV (Nov. 1960).

Mitani Sachiko. '*Sanuki no Suke Nikki* dembon ni tsuite', *Heian bungaku kenkyū*, vols. XXXVII and XXXVIII (Nov. 1966 and June 1967).

Miyazaki Shōhei. '*Sanuki no Suke Nikki* ni tsuite no shōron', *Kokugo to kokubungaku*, vol. XLI (Mar. 1964).

———. '*Sanuki no Suke Nikki* no [Hitachidono] ni tsuite', *Kokubungaku*, vol. XIV (Nov. 1969).

——. 'Ōchō nikki no jōshu to seikatsu—jōryū nikki no tenkai—*Sanuki no Suke Nikki*', *Kokubungaku kaishaku to kanshō*, vol. XXXVII (April 1972).

Morimoto Motoko. '*Sanuki no Suke Nikki*—shi wo gyōshi shite', *Kokubungaku kaishaku to kanshō* (Jan. 1954).

Morita Kenkichi. '*Sanuki no Suke Nikki* no seiritsu', *Kokugo kokubun*, vol. XXII, no. 1 (Jan. 1963).

Moriya Seigo. 'Horikawa mikado no kōkyū—*Sanuki no Suke Nikki* keisei no haikei', *Heian bungaku kenkyū*, vol. XLVII (Nov. 1971).

Motoida Shigemi. '*Sanuki no Suke Nikki* shikai—"Kisaragi ni narite" no jō ni tsuite', *Jimbun ronkyū*, vol. XVI, no. 2 (July 1965).

Ōki Fujio. '*Sanuki no Suke Nikki* tokoro—dokoro—zenchūkai no kankō ni saishite', *Kokugo kokubun*, vol. XXXVIII (Nov. 1969).

Ōtomo Yōko. '*Sanuki no Suke Nikki* sakusha kōshō—Fujiwara no Nagako, Toshinari kyō no koto ni tsuite', *Joshi daikokubun*, vol. X (Oct. 1958).

Sakurai Hideshi. '*Sanuki no Suke kō*', *Kokugakuin zasshi*, vol. XV, nos. 7 and 8 (July and Aug. 1909).

*Sanuki no Suke Nikki*, in *Gunsho ruijū* series, vol. XI, Tokyo: Keizai Zasshisha, 1894.

*Sanuki no Suke Nikki*, in *Heianchō nikkishū: zen*, Tokyo: Yūhōdō Shoten, 1927.

Tamai Kōsuke. *Sanuki no Suke Nikki* in *Nihon koten zensho* series, Tokyo: Asahi Shimbunsha, 1964.

——. *Sanuki no Suke Nikki tsūshaku*, Tokyo: Ikuei Shoin, 1936.

——. *Sanuki no Suke Nikki zenchūkai*, Tokyo: Yūseidō, 1969.

——. '*Sanuki no Suke Nikki* chū no jimbutsu', *Shigaku zasshi*, vol. XLI, no. 11 (Nov. 1930).

——. '*Sanuki no Suke Nikki* sakusha ni tsuite', *Shigaku zasshi*, vol. XL, no. 9 (Sept. 1929).

GENERAL WORKS
Primary sources in Japanese

*Chōshūki*, in *Shiryō taisei*, vols. VI-VII, Tokyo: Naigai Shoseki, 1934.

*Chūyūki*, in *Shiryō taisei*, vols. VIII-XIV, Tokyo: Naigai Shoseki, 1934-5.

*Denreki*, in *Dainihon kokiroku*, Tokyo: Iwanami Shoten, 1960.

*Eiga Monogatari*, in *Nihon koten bungaku taikei*, vols. LXXV-LXXVII, Tokyo: Iwanami Shoten, 1964.

*Fukuro Sōshi*, in *Zoku gunsho ruijū*, vol. XVI, part 2, Tokyo: Zoku Gunsho Ruijū Kanseikai, 1931.

*Gukanshō*, in *Nihon koten bungaku taikei*, vol. LXXXVI, Tokyo: Iwanami Shoten, 1967.

*Heian Kamakura shikashū*, in *Nihon koten bungaku taikei*, vol. LXXX, Tokyo: Iwanami Shoten, 1964.

*Heike Monogatari*, in *Nihon koten bungaku taikei*, vol. XXXII, Tokyo: Iwanami Shoten, 1959.

*Honchō Shojaku Mokuroku*, in *Gunsho ruijū*, vol. XVIII, Tokyo: Keizai Zasshisha, 1896.

*Ima Kagami*, in *Nihon bungaku taikei*, vol. XII, Tokyo: Kokumin Tosho, 1926.

*Jinnō Shōtōki*, in *Nihon koten bungaku taikei*, vol. XX, Tokyo: Iwanami Shoten, 1965.

*Kimpishō*, in *Shinshū kōgaku sōsho*, vol. V, Tokyo: Kōbunko, 1927.

*Kojidan*, in *Kokushi taikei*, vol. XVIII, Tokyo: Yoshikawa kōbunkan, 1932.

*Kokon Chomonjū*, in *Nihon koten bungaku taikei*, vol. LXXXIV, Tokyo: Iwanami Shoten, 1966.

*Konjaku Monogatari Shū*, in *Nihon koten bungaku taikei*, vol. XXVI, Tokyo: Iwanami Shoten, 1963.

*Makura no Sōshi, Murasaki Shikibu Nikki*, in *Nihon koten bungaku taikei*, vol. XIX, Tokyo: Iwanami Shoten, 1965.

*Mumyōshō*, in *Gunsho ruijū*, vol. X, Tokyo: Keizai Zasshisha, 1896.

*Ōkagami*, in *Nihon koten bungaku taikei*, vol. XXI, Tokyo: Iwanami Shoten, 1960.

*Ryōjin Hisshō*, in *Nihon koten bungaku taikei*, vol. LXXIII, Tokyo: Iwanami Shoten, 1965.

*Sandaishū no Aida no Koto*, in *Gunsho ruijū*, vol. X, Tokyo: Keizai Zasshisha, 1894.

*Sompi Bummyaku*, in *Kokushi taikei*, vols. LVIII-LX, Tokyo: Yoshikawa Kōbunkan, 1961–2.

*Tenso Reiki Shokushō Roku*, in *Gunsho ruijū*, vol. II, Tokyo: Keizai Zasshisha, 1894.

*Tosa Nikki, Kagerō Nikki, Izumi Shikibu Nikki, Sarashina Nikki*, in *Nihon koten bungaku taikei*, vol. XX, Tokyo: Iwanami Shoten, 1965.

*Uji Shūi Monogatari*, in *Nihon koten bungaku taikei*, vol. XXVII, Tokyo: Iwanami Shoten, 1960.

*Uta-awase Shū*, in *Nihon koten bungaku taikei*, vol. LXXIV, Tokyo: Iwanami Shoten, 1965.

*Zoku Kojidan*, in *Gunsho ruijū*, vol. XVIII, Tokyo: Keizai Zasshisha, 1894.

*Waka kashū bu*, in *Gunsho ruijū*, vols. IX-X, Tokyo: Keizai Zasshisha, 1894.

Translations

Cranston, Edwin A. *The Izumi Shikibu Diary—a Romance of the Heian Court*, Cambridge, Mass: Harvard University Press, 1969.

Katō Bunnō. *Myōhō-Renge-Kyō, The Sutra of the Lotus Flower of the Wonderful Law*, revised by W. E. Soothill and W. Schiffer, Tokyo: Risshō Kōseikai, 1971.

Keene, Donald. *Essays in Idleness, the Tsurezuregusa of Kenkō*, New York: Columbia University Press, 1967.

Miner, Earl Roy. *Japanese Poetic Diaries*, Berkeley: University of Calfornia Press, 1969. Includes translation of *Tosa Nikki* and *Izumi Shikibu Nikki*.

Morris, Ivan. *The Pillow Book of Sei Shōnagon*, New York: Columbia University Press, 1967.

——. *As I Crossed a Bridge of Dreams: Recollections of a Woman in Eleventh-century Japan*, London: Oxford University Press, 1971. Translation of *Sarashina Nikki*.

Seidensticker, Edward. *The Gossamer Years, the Diary of a Noblewoman of Heian Japan*, Tokyo: Tuttle, 1964.

——. 'The *Kagerō Nikki*: Journal of a 10th Century Noblewoman', *Transactions of the Asiatic Society of Japan*, Third Series, vol. IV (June 1955).

Wilson, William R. *Hōgen Monogatari, Tale of the Disorder of Hōgen*, Tokyo: Sophia University Press, 1971.

Yamagiwa, Joseph K. *The Ōkagami, a Japanese historical tale*, London: George Allen and Unwin, 1967.

Secondary sources

Akagi Shizuko. 'Shirakawa-in to Horikawa tennō—insei shoki no in to tennō', *Shintōgaku*, no. 53 (May 1967).

Arimoto Minoru. *Ōchō seiji no seisui*, in *Nihon rekishi kōza*, vol. II, Tokyo:Tokyo Daigaku, 1964.

Fujiki Kunihiko. *Nihon zenshi*, vol. III, *Kodai*, vol. II, Tokyo: Tokyo Daigaku, 1962.

Fujioka Sakutarō. *Kokubungaku zenshi: Heianchō hen*, Tokyo: Kaiseikan, 1906.

Hagitani Boku. 'Chōji gannen gogatsu nijū rokunichi sakone gonchūjō Toshitada uta-awase', in *Heianchō uta-awase taisei*, vol. V, Tokyo: privately published, 1961.

Hall, John Whitney. *Government and Local Power in Japan 500–1700, a study based on Bizen province*, Princeton, N.J.: Princeton University Press, 1966.

Hashimoto Fumio. 'Inseiki kadan no ikkōsatsu—Fujiwara no Toshitada no shōgai wo megutte', *Shoryōbu kiyō*, vol. X (Oct. 1958).

——. 'Minamoto no Kunizane to *Renjaku hyakushu*—Horikawa-in kadan no shūen', *Shoryōbu kiyō*, vol. XII (Oct. 1960).

Hayashima Kyōshō (ed.). *Japanese-English Buddhist Dictionary*, Tokyo: Daitō, 1965.

Hayashiya Tatsusaburō. *Kodai kokka no kaitai*, Tokyo: Tokyo Daigaku, 1955.

Hisamatsu Sen'ichi. *Nihon bungaku shi: chūko*, Tokyo: Shibundō, 1959.

——. *Nihon bungaku shi: chūsei*, Tokyo: Shibundō, 1959.

Hurst, G. Cameron III. 'The Development of the *Insei*: A Problem in Japanese History and Historiography' in Hall, John W. and Mass, Jeffrey P. (eds.), *Medieval Japan, Essays in Institutional History*, New Haven and London: Yale University Press, 1974.

——. '*Insei*, Abdicated Sovereigns in the Politics of Late Heian Japan, 1086–1185', Ph.D. diss., Columbia University, 1972.

——. 'The Reign of Go-Sanjō and the Revival of Imperial Power', *Monumenta Nipponica*, vol. XXVII (1972).

——. 'The Structure of the Heian Court: Some Thoughts on the Nature of "Familial Authority" in Heian Japan' in Hall, John W. and Mass, Jeffrey P. (eds.), *Medieval Japan, Essays in Institutional History*, New Haven and London: Yale University Press, 1974.

Ikeda Kikan. *Heian jidai bungaku gaisetsu*, Tokyo: Yakumo Shoten, 1944.

——. *Kyūtei joryū nikki bungaku*, Tokyo: Shinbundō, 1965. First published 1927.

——. *Kyūtei to koten bungaku*, Tokyo: Kōfūkan, 1943.

——. *Monogatari bungaku*, in *Nihon bungaku kyōyō kōza*, vol. VI, Tokyo: Shibundō, 1951.

——. 'Nihon bungaku, shomoku kaisetsu 2: Heian jidai ge', in *Iwanami kōza Nihon bungaku*, vols. VIII and XII, Tokyo: Iwanami Shoten, 1932.

Imai Takuji. *Heian jidai nikki bungaku no kenkyū*, Tokyo: Meiji Shoin, 1957.

Ishimoda Shō. *Kodai makki seijishi josetsu*, Tokyo: Miraisha, 1964.

Itō Yoshio (ed.). *Waka bungaku daijiten*, Tokyo: Meiji Shoin, 1962.

Kodama Kōta (ed.). *Shiryō ni yoru Nihon no ayumi, Kodai hen*, Tokyo: Yoshikawa kōbunkan, 1960.

Kōno Fusao. 'Shirakawa-in no kinshindan no ichikōsatu', *Nihon rekishi*, no. 145 (July 1960).

Kuroda Toshio. 'Chūsei no kokka to tennō, in *Iwanami kōza Nihon rekishi*, vol. VI, *Chūsei*, vol. II, Tokyo: Iwanami Shoten, 1963.

Matsumura Hiroji. *Eiga monogatari no kenkyū*, Tokyo: Tōkō Shoin, 1956.

Miura Hiroyuki. *Zoku hōseishi no kenkyū*, Tokyo: Iwanami Shoten, 1925.

Morita Kenkichi. 'Nikki bungaku to dokusha', *Heian bungaku kenkyū*, vol. XXVI (June 1961).

Nishishita Kyōichi. 'Heianchō no nikki kikō,' in *Iwanami kōza Nihon bungaku*, vol. VIII, Tokyo: Iwanami Shoten, 1932.

Oka Kazuo. *Genji monogatari no kisoteki kenkyū*, Tokyo: Tōkyōdō, 1955.

Okuno Takahiro. *Kōshitsu gokeizaishi no kenkyū*, Tokyo: Unebi Shoin, 1942.

Takeuchi Rizō. *Bushi no tōjō*, in *Nihon no rekishi*, vol. VI, Tokyo: Chūō Kōronsha, 1965.

——. 'Insei no seiritsu', in *Iwanami kōza Nihon rekishi*, vol. IV, *Kodai*, vol. IV, Tokyo: Iwanami Shoten, 1962.

Tamai Kōsuke. 'Kamakura jidai no nikki kikō', in *Iwanami kōza Nihon bungaku*, vol. XII, Tokyo: Iwanami Shoten, 1932.

——. *Nikki bungaku gaisetsu*, Tokyo: Meguro Shoten, 1945.

——. *Nikki bungaku no kenkyū*, Tokyo: Hanawa Shobō, 1965.

Tsuji Zennosuke. *Nihon bukkyō shi*, vol. I, *Jōsei hen*, Tokyo: Iwanami Shoten, 1960.

Wada Hidematsu. 'Rekishijō ni okeru menoto no seiryoku', *Kokugakuin zasshi*, vol. XVIII, no. 1 (1912).

# INDEX